# THE MODERN MAN'S CODE TO MANHOOD

## HOW TO WIN THE WAR WITH YOURSELF, BECOME EMOTIONALLY INTELLIGENT & MASTER YOURSELF

## BRENDONGIEBEL

Advanced Men's Development

**The Modern Man's Code To Manhood**

First Print - August 2022

## This Book is Dedicated to

Everyone who has shaped me into the man I am today.

Those whose stories you will hear in this book.

To my mother and father for the lessons they have taught me.

My past, present, and future clients are the reason I keep doing what I'm doing.

Without them, Advanced Men's Development would not exist.

And this guide for the Modern Man would not matter.

Every man I will help and serve is why I continue to live by this Code.

My hope is that you take this and become an Advanced Man just like me.

Are you ready to become the most Advanced Man you can be?

# THE MODERN MAN'S CODE
## TO MANHOOD

# THE INTRODUCTION

Dear Brother,

Your decision to purchase this book may turn out to be the smartest decision you've ever made.

Look, you are here right now, and you have gotten to where you are by doing whatever it is that you have been doing.

You are about to read this book and embark on this journey, but the reality is that I don't know who you are.

I don't know what you do.

I don't even know if you are a man; maybe you are a woman.

I really don't know anything about you.

But I do know that you are searching for something.

Maybe your life isn't working right now.

Maybe your life isn't moving in the direction you want it to go.

Maybe you don't even know what direction you want to or should go.

Maybe you are struggling to obtain the things you desire in life, or perhaps you do not even want to live anymore.

If any of these are you, my brother, welcome.

You might be someone for whom none of the above resonates,

Maybe your life is starting to become boring, dull, and it doesn't excite you anymore,
or maybe you know there's more out there for you, but you just can't find that place.

Again, welcome.

The Modern Man's Code isn't designed for perfect men with perfect lives.

It's designed to meet you where you are currently standing and grow with you through this journey.

I've been in all those places, and I've emerged from each of them realising one thing…

The reality, sometimes a harsh reality to realise, is that you have created the life you are currently living. If you think that it has been created by some other person, force, or series of events, then you are living in someone else's reality, not your own.

You have given ALL your power away.

What you should also realise is that you have the power to change your reality.

The only person that can ultimately save you is yourself.

Yes, my friend, you have that power!

This book and this brotherhood will offer you the help and guidance to achieve it.

It took me six months to write this book, but the MMC (that's short for Modern Man's Code, just for future reference) has been years in the making.

From the struggles to the successes,

The wins to the losses,

From the victories to the defeats,

From the pain to the pleasure,

And from the agony and heartache,

The MMC has been forged as we know it today.

I can tell you now that this journey has been as hard as hell for me, and looking back on it,
I'm not sure I would have gone through with it had I known how much effort it would take.

But I knew something was missing in my life, and I wasn't going to stop until I found it.

I could tell you about my life and what I've been through,
I could tell you about my struggles and the pain and suffering I have dealt with.

But that doesn't mean much to you.

You have your own struggles, painful experiences, and at times, seemingly endless suffering.

Listening to my struggle is not what this is about.

The experiences that are your past are going to stay there.

As you move through this book and implement each aspect of it, your life will begin to shift.

Others will ask what you have been doing, they will notice your transformations, and they will see the life that you are starting to build around yourself.

My only hope is that you can see this too.

And you take all this on board and strive to be the best man you can be.

Your mind will be opened to the new possibilities of living the way inside the AMD brotherhood.

Living this way is not an easy task. It's not something you just read once and forget about, and it's not something that will change you by merely only reading it.

You must be ready to implement everything inside and get real, raw, and honest about who you are, where you are, and who you want to become.

This book isn't for the faint-hearted. This is only for a select group of men who are willing to put in the effort to live an extraordinary life and achieve greatness.

If you do the hard things in life, your life will be easy.

If you do the easy things in life, your life will be hard.

My journey all started with a decision to make some radical changes in my life,
regardless of what I had to do and the willingness to never give up until I reached that place.

I was at rock bottom and had to deal with some dark, dark shit.

I had to rise out of the pit of sorrow I'd put myself in.

But you don't have to wait until you hit rock bottom to start rising out of your hole.

All you need to do is make the decision to start,

And you can do that right now.

Everything that you want and desire in life is possible for you,
and it's not that these things don't exist already.

It comes down to the fact that you are simply not yet aware of their existence.

Or that they actually might be possible for you.

I realise this might seem a bit far-fetched or even impossible for you right now,
let me remind you that you are the creator of your reality.

And you've spent an entire lifetime creating your current reality, which is primarily constructed on your beliefs.

Most of them are unconscious to you, they are limiting you, and they have been for a long time.

So how do you achieve and create a new reality?

Your ability to have faith in the unforeseen,
to have faith in yourself and have confidence in what you can achieve.

Some of you will take this by the horns while having this faith,
and transform your lives at a radical pace.

Others will not see the same results.

This all comes down to one thing:

You must decide on this path for yourself and not for anybody else's benefit.

If you don't choose to do it for yourself, you will fail.

This path is not guaranteed to work if you are not willing to put in the work and do it for yourself.

My hope is for you to achieve the transformational process of the MMC, which has been experienced in my own life and the lives of so many men who have embarked on this journey before you.

Now it's your turn.

Welcome, my brother.


*Brendon Giebel*


Founder of AMD

Creator of The AMD App

Author of The Modern Man's Code

Human Behaviour Expert, Life Strategist & Speaker

# FOREWORD

## Kim Morrison

This easy-to-read, wisdom-rich, and personally written book could not be more timely. The teachings and insights are powerful and timeless. All men from all walks of life need to read this book and take what it says to heart.

But let's get frank. Mental health is at crisis point. According to Beyond Blue, every day in Australia seven men will take their life, with men three times more likely to die by suicide than anything else. What is also astounding is evidence indicates men are far less likely to seek help for mental health conditions than women. One in seven men will experience depression and or anxiety in one year.

I am married to a beautiful man who sadly, has experienced falling to the depths of depression and guilt, shame and remorse and deep sadness. Thankfully, over a long period of time, and with the help of many, we crawled out of this hideous rock-bottom pit together. I do not take any of the perils of mental health lightly. I wish these statistics for men were not true. And I wish we had had this book for my husband and I as we clumsily navigated our way through that time.

When Brendon Giebel asked me to write the foreword for 'The Modern Man's Code To Manhood', I may have questioned why he would ask a woman to write it for a book that is really targeting men?

As I read each page glued to the simple yet profound advice, I realised that this, whilst it is indeed written for men, we need to get real and realise most men who find themselves falling into the mosh-pit of life will most likely not even see a book like this, let alone read it.

So, this book needs to be read by all women of all walks of life too. We all need to read it to know there is a way out and to be that guide for those who think they can't.

Being a good man; a man who lives and breathes his truth, is undoubtedly a man who embodies the title of King. Being a King means creating an unshakable alliance with yourself. This book is the pathway, a code and the ultimate step-by-step process to bring you home to you.

What helps to make this book so credible is that the author is upfront in sharing his own remarkable story. He acknowledges that a happy life is not about having the perfect life or about being the perfect man. It is about getting real, being open and honest about where you are right now.

It is about taking back your power and realising you have the ability to change your reality in every moment of every day.

This book offers the ideal support to grow through whatever it is that you go through at any stage in your life.

With a female lens, I realise whilst we may have slightly different wants and needs, or have different skills or talents, ultimately men and women are pursuing similar things. Through my own research and witnessing my husband and son's journeys closely, I realise men ultimately want to;

~ Love and be loved
~ Feel good about who they are
~ Be able to provide and protect with courage and strength
~ Have a positive relationship with self

~ Have meaningful connection with others

~ Appreciate the importance of mental health

~ Understand their emotions and why they do what they do

~ Change the debilitating, self-sabotaging story they may be telling themselves into a desired and powerful version of the story

~ Feel they are capable and worthy of being a King and...

~ Know what they need to bravely man up, continuously show up and never give up

The Modern Man's Code To Manhood offers a pathway, a guide, it offers results-driven, actionable steps and most of all, it offers hope.

Brendon carefully and thoughtfully shows men how to be the master of life's fate, instead of sitting fearfully and or angrily on the sidelines or getting whiplashed by reacting to the volatility of life's challenges in detrimental ways. He provides sensible insights that will keep men from making the same mistakes or having the same limiting thoughts over and over.

Even better, he explains what actions to take - such as the Daily 8 – that can lay the foundations for helping men to rise into the King they were born to be.

The Modern Man's Code To Manhood is not an end in and of itself, but it is a crucial aspect of achieving a rich and purposeful life. If you are willing to follow this life-changing code, if you are willing to surrender and shine the light on what may feel dark and heavy, you will find your way, and you will reap the rewards.

As Buddha so eloquently says, 'A man may conquer a million men in battle, but one who conquers himself is indeed the greatest of conquerors.'

The Modern Man's Code To Manhood is your new coat of armour, your secret weapon. It is your opportunity to face rock bottom and a willingness to fight for your right to be the powerful modern man you were destined to be.

There is no accident you are reading this right now. It shows you are ready. And it could be in a way you never thought possible.

Kim Morrison

# Contents

# THE MODERN MAN'S CODE TO MANHOOD

## How To Win The War With Yourself, Become Emotionally Intelligent & Master Yourself

# 1

# PART I: THE OVERVIEW

## THE FOUNDATION

*"To see things in the seed, that is genius."*
## - Lao Tzu

Without this Framework or Code and the story of how it came about, nothing inside it would make sense or even be possible. So let me start by describing the foundation on which the Code as we know it today was built.

One evening in 2013, I lay diagonally across my bed, which had only recently become empty again for the second time in as many years. I could feel the cold air and slight mist from the storm outside blowing through the screen window beside me. It was peaceful, being there in the dark while hearing the rain falling just outside the window. It took me back to my childhood, where I would sit and just watch the rain falling outside. You could smell the freshness that the rain would bring. But this time, though, something was different.

As I lay there, I contemplated my life, not about whether to live or not, but more along the lines of what it was that I genuinely wanted to do with my life. I didn't know it then, but this was one of the first internal deciding factors in my journey's commencement. It's not very often that a man allows himself to sit there by himself, in silence, and think.

The more I thought about who I was and what I wanted from my life, the clearer this became. I lived my life within a fake reality, trying to live a life that wasn't the reality I was actually living. I realised I was telling stories and lying to myself and everyone else in my life. Why? Because it made me feel better about myself if others thought it seemed better from the outside. I thought the more people who thought my life was great, the more convinced I'd be.

It didn't quite work out that way, and after that night of thought, sadly, it all faded away the next morning.

It wasn't until a few years later, and after some dark periods and intense dark phases in my life, this thought of not living the life true to who I was, popped its head up again for me to hear and see.

The reality was that I hated my life at this time, and I didn't want to face the truth about my life. I would make up some bullshit story about how great my life was to make me feel and look good from the outside, but on the inside, I was imploding! I even got a small slice of satisfaction from telling people these stories, although it never lasted very long.

### The Big Pretender

I was pretending to be someone that I wasn't. It was doing nothing but causing me tremendous amounts of stress because I couldn't live up to my own bullshit stories that I was telling. I was being driven into the ground, literally into the ground, trying to cover up my darkness and reality.

Ever had that feeling? All excited and pumped up on the outside but slowly dying on the inside. There comes the point where no matter how many energy drinks you consume, how many coffees you drink or how many drugs you take, nothing will keep you going. Nothing will excite you anymore, and nothing is worth it anymore.

What is one question most people get asked each day? 'How are you?'

And what's the most common response? 'I'm good.' Every single day, it's the same response, and I was the same. I really wanted to say, 'I feel like shit, and I hate my life.' But we can't tell anyone that. It goes against our conditioning as a man raised in today's society. Everyone would just tell me to stop whinging or even just 'man up'... I remember being called and also calling other boys at school pussies if they cried.

### The Foundation of Truth

As we head into the evolution of Part One of the MMC, you'll come to realise that the foundation of the Code is your ability as a man to face the facts of your own life and begin to live a life based on the foundation of the truth. And your ability to learn what it takes for you to start telling the truth.

Allowing you to see your life as just the way it is, with no feelings or stories attached; it just is what it is. This gives you the clarity to ask yourself the hard questions and hear the hard answers from that voice inside you. It's the voice that comes from the heart.

'Is my life working?' 'no,' ok great... let's look at the facts.

'Why is it not working?' 'well, it's not working here, and it's not working here, and it's not really working here.'

From this place, you can begin to move from a place of powerless to a place of power. The foundation of the facts allows the truth to ultimately set you free.

### Eradicating the Liar Within

This goes deeper than just affirming to always accept the truth and to stop lying. Sitting there saying, 'I do not lie,' is a lie in itself. We are men, and we lie, just like anyone else on this earth. We always have lied and always will. Realising this allows you to understand that telling a lie and the amount you tell ultimately comes down to your decision. But being in a place where a lie doesn't even become a thought anymore is the target. A massive flow of power shifts at this point, from a man being a story-telling liar to becoming a king in his world and building his kingdom.

There were a few long years where this 'I'm not a liar' story was something I was still trying to figure out. In a society trained to be liars, it's hard for a man to be able to tell the truth. So, I started down this path of what it really meant to start telling the truth. It was a path that only I seemed to be on. Except for a few, everyone around me would not accept me when I said or did what I felt.

In a world full of men who tell lies all the time, I would start to tell the truth in everything I did. If I messed up, 'yes, it was me.' I would have other people saying to me, 'Brendon, why would you tell them that?'. They didn't understand at the time, and, don't get me wrong, I was questioning the same things.

### Without the Lies Comes Nothing to Lie About

I speak about this power that comes from telling the truth, which is an incredible power in itself. But the real power comes to you when knowing that if you put yourself in a position where you might lie about something in the future, it affects the decision you make in the current moment. It's an internal shift in how you start to live based on the foundation of the truth.

The foundation based on telling the truth liberates us from lying to ourselves, lying to others, and lying to the world. Removing all the fear behind being found out and exposed, never having to remember a story that was made up, and never having to worry about 'I hope I don't get caught.'

### Open the Gates to Freedom

Nobody in my world taught me that being brutally honest and not lying would be the gateway to my freedom. That my capability to tell the truth would open these gates, and it will open yours too if you decide to be honest and tell the truth.

I realised very fast that when equipped with this book and everything inside it, I would feel like the most powerful man when I walked into any room. Maybe not the loudest and maybe not the 'life of the party', but I was able to say things that others wouldn't have even thought of saying. I would have the capacity to say yes to everything I wanted and no to everything I didn't. I was able to be real, raw, and honest in everything I said and did, and with things that others would never have had any means to express.

Now it's time. I have set the story and the foundation for what the Modern Man's Code is all about. We're going to cover everything: from The Challenging Evolution, The Path, The Possibilities, and The Purpose, all the way to The Facts, Feelings, and Fibs, one at a time, each in their own chapter. We are getting you prepared for your new reality inside the AMD Brotherhood.

## KEY POINTS

**POINT #1:** Without this Framework or Code and the story of how it came about, nothing inside it would make sense or even be possible.

**POINT #2:** I was pretending to be someone that I wasn't. It was doing nothing but causing me tremendous amounts of stress because I couldn't live up to my own bullshit stories that I was telling.

**POINT #3:** The foundation of the Code is your ability as a man to face the facts of your own life and begin to live a life based on the foundation of the truth. And your ability to learn what it takes for you to start telling the truth.

**POINT #4:** The real power comes to you when knowing that if you put yourself in a position where you might lie about something in the future, it affects the decision you make in the current moment.

# 2

## THE POSSIBILITIES

*"Probable impossibilities are to be preferred to improbable possibilities."*
**- Aristotle**

Long before the creation of AMD or even the first thought of finally finding liberation in my own life, it all started with a possibility. Everything that happens in this world, everything that becomes something, is all backed by a possibility. Taking this a step further, a possibility is backed by a belief.

At some point in your life, you must take a stand and challenge your current foundational beliefs. The reality is that most of the time, we live in a world backed by the outdated views, ideas, and opinions of older men and women rather than our own.

I studied The *Tao Te Ching*, an ancient Chinese philosophy. The *Tao Te Ching*, which translates as *The Book of the Way*, and its philosophy of Taoism, are based on simplicity, patience, and compassion.[1] I found inside of this that there is a process in which everything in the Universe happens, named the Tao. Not only is the Tao everything that is currently in existence, but it's everything that doesn't exist too. These things that don't currently exist actually do exist, just not within our worldview or current set of beliefs.

Without any sort of belief, nothing will ever be possible. This lack of belief limits us and makes the process of becoming who we want to become so damn hard. Look around the space you are in right now; nearly everything in that space would not be here if it were not for someone having had a belief that it might be possible first. Your phone became a possibility out of a belief, your furniture became a possibility out of a belief, and landing on the moon became a possibility out of a belief.

**The 4-Minute Mile**

For hundreds of years, the 4-min mile was thought to be an impossible barrier that could never be broken. It was deemed to be humanly impossible. Many doctors and scientists stated that your body would shut down before achieving such a feat. That is, apart from one man named Roger Bannister. He believed it could be done, so he trained and trained and trained until he became the first man ever to succeed in this unattainable achievement. He came in at a time of 3:59.4.[2] Why? Because he had the belief that he could.

What happened after he broke this record changed how people saw beliefs and possibilities. Just 46 days after Roger broke this record, another person broke the once deemed impossible task; they saw the possibilities. Now it's been broken by over 1,500 runners, all stemming from this one belief that Roger had all those years ago.

*'When I Let Go Of What I Am, I Become What I Might Be.'* – Lao Tzu

Letting go of your current beliefs is the gateway to new possibilities. So, I ask you: are your beliefs allowing you to experience your possibilities? Does your potential equal your reality? Are your beliefs hiding the possibilities, hiding the *Tao*?

Far too often, men end up in situations where they are lost and searching for something greater, knowing there is something more out there, although it can't be found or even defined. I speak with men daily who struggle to tell me what they are experiencing or what they want their life to look like in the future. We tend to look up to others who have more money, more women, more cars, a better life, and a life of abundance, wishing and wanting to have all those things too. But that's where it stops, at a wish. We don't believe that we will ever be able to achieve this, and because of this, we struggle to imagine it would ever be possible.

All those dreams we see and have, get pushed away, hidden, and deemed impossible. I want to open your mind to the possibility that nothing is impossible. Just as stated by the Tao, everything exists. I have no doubt in my mind that there is a better version of you inside.

'He's a better provider.'

'He's a better boyfriend & husband.'

'He's in better shape.'

'He makes more money.'

'He has better sex.'

'He has better relationships.'

That man, the Advanced Man, is already inside of you. The problem is that he is stuck behind the belief of impossibility. I can tell you that nobody ever achieved anything they thought was impossible. I want you to consider what might be possible for you if you removed the barrier of impossibility. If you take on the Taoist belief that everything exists, even if you don't know it does, let yourself open your mind. Allow and give yourself permission to let go... of who you currently are for you to become the man you WANT to become.

**Are You Ready to Pay The Price?**

If I had known how much pain I was going to go through, how much money I was going to spend, how much work, blood, sweat, and tears it was going to take for me to get to the place I am right now, I promise you that I would have never embarked on this journey. I would have quit, fallen into the belief of impossibility, and said, 'Screw this, I'm out,' like the night I nearly did.

In 2014, I was working FIFO on a small Island called Barrow Island off the coast of Western Australia.[3] I had been here for about 9 months, and this is where I had the lowest and darkest time of my life. I would go through cycles of binge eating 4 or 5 plates of food to starving myself for days trying to make up for it. Alongside this, I would work out twice daily, before and after work.

For some weird reason, inflicting pain on myself this way brought a tiny bit of happiness into my life. I fully believe the gym was the only thing that kept me going, which is why I believe it's imperative everyone should be doing some form of exercise every day, but more on that in a later chapter.

During my time on this island, my roster was 26 days on and 9 off. Every time I flew back, I wished the plane would crash and it would be over. I never blamed the site, FIFO or anything as it wasn't the cause; it just amplified the problems within myself. If I hadn't experienced this at this time, it would have happened later on in my life.

In month 11, I was on my R&R break, and it was a Wednesday night. I lived in an apartment building on level 7, but this night was like no other. It was about 9 o'clock at night. I was sitting outside with a beer in my hand. I had tears running down my face, and I'd had enough. I was done. I was out.

I got up, walked to the edge of my balcony, and looked down to find a spot that was the full 7 stories down: a tiny spot about 2m square. I'd put my hands on the rail and put one leg onto the rail until I had the most amazing thing happen to me.

Still to this day, I have no idea where this came from, but all I heard was, 'Are you really going to give up this easy?'

I listened, and at that moment, I decided that I would commit to making things start to get better.

Just like any great journey, it all begins with that one first step.[4] It took me four years to dig myself out of my own dark hole and free myself from my own thoughts. It took another four years to look, search, and discover what it meant to be a man and build a kingdom. I'm not there yet, there will always be a step higher, but I can tell you now that the possibilities are endless when you adapt to living by the MMC, join us inside the AMD Brotherhood and become an Advanced Man.

I'm going to make it very clear that this is not something you go through just reading, listening to, or watching, like we tend to do when we start a new program or system, just getting through everything and then hoping it will work. Getting to the end and hoping it has transformed our lives. There is no end to this; it's not something you do for 30 days and then fall straight back into your old way of life.

This is a new way to live, a daily set of tasks designed to expand your life as a whole, taking you to all new heights and possibilities. This isn't about just improving one area of your life. There are plenty of men out there who don't need any help at all in some areas of their life. You might be a man in great shape with a great body, but your relationships and social life suck. You might be a man who makes a ton of money but has the health of an eighty-year-old. You might be a man who is a great father and husband but cannot get anywhere with his finances. You might be a man who has a great spiritual connection and is in tune with your body but can never find a lasting relationship. These are all examples of men who are well trained in one area but lacking in others. Also known as a one-dimensional man.

I'm not going to sit here and say this will be easy, nor will I say that it's going to be for everyone. There's a select group of men who desire to live up to their potential, build their dream life and be and live the life of a king. At first – and it was the same for me – completing your Daily 8 (Part IV) every single day can feel like a chore. I can tell you that once you start, there's no going back. You will not want to miss a day; you will feel like shit the day you don't do your 8. The Daily 8 will no longer feel like a chore but something you look forward to doing each and every day.

## My Own World Results

There was a time when I would switch between intense workouts and all-out binge eating at dinner, which only fuelled a downward spiral as I went from an eating event to an excessive workout in an attempt to 'make up' for it. While my mind was hurting and my body was in pain, I would push myself to find the 'high' that comes from the release of endorphins after exercise. The experiences I had when I was abusing my body in the gym actually made me happy, and it felt like the only place that could make me feel this way. By contrast, I'm now in the best physical and mental shape of my life. My health is on point, and I rarely have a day when I don't feel energised.

I became a man who went from being delusional about my spiritual wellbeing and mental health to longing for the chance to get into a deep meditative state and have my mind mentally tough enough to take anything on. I went from being lost, not knowing what I wanted to do, who I wanted to be, or even who I was, to knowing my purpose. I know now when that voice inside my mind is talking, and instead of shutting it off, I listen to what it has to say. That doesn't mean I believe it or take it on board; I often just let those thoughts past. Because that's all they are, just thoughts. If you don't put a meaning to it, it will stay a thought and just pass.

I went from being a guy who was shy and afraid to talk to females without having ten shots of Dutch Courage to a man living with close and intimate relationships with essentially whoever I wish. I went from a guy who would lie, expecting partners to be perfect, even though I didn't have to be. I was self-centred, being the opposite of assertive and getting angry over tiny things, which drove females away from me, to now being the man women want to hang out with, assertive and compassionate, and living in abundance.

I went from empty bank accounts while starting a construction business, living a life where work was a constant task and hanging out only on rare days off, to my life now, being the founder of Advanced Men's Development with huge passion. This is not a job for me, and I have total clarity about where I'm going and who I am becoming. The satisfaction I get from seeing the transformation in my clients far outweighs any bridge I would have built back in the construction game.

Being ignorant when it came to stress and believing that it didn't happen to me only drove me to experience completely drunken tidal waves of emotion that came as a release to stress. Now that I'm able to recognise this stress and let go of it quickly, I can go out with friends and not feel the need to drink alcohol, and if I do drink, it doesn't lead to waking up with the feeling of 'What happened to me last night?'

None of what you have just read is intended for me to brag or say, 'Look at me'. The message I want to share is simple: these are the possibilities that are out there when you decide to commit fully to living by the MMC. I speak of these possibilities being available to you because they *are* already possible for you. You just need to be awakened to these possibilities so you can grasp the belief of the man you will be and the life you will build.

### It Starts With You

The most famous quote from the *Tao Te Ching* states, 'Your journey of a thousand miles begins with a single step.' If you look at this journey as a whole, odds are you will get overwhelmed and give up. It will become a question of 'How am I going to pull this off?' As you work through this book, it will become clear what possibilities might open up for you. I am not forcing you to do anything here. I am not telling you that you need to do anything here. I am not telling you that you must follow what I say. All I am giving you is the chance to take on this system, as I have, and become someone you never thought possible. The decision is ultimately yours.

## KEY POINTS

**POINT #1:** Everything that happens in this world, everything that becomes something, is all backed by a possibility.

**POINT #2:** Letting go of your current beliefs is the gateway to new possibilities.

**POINT #3:** This is a new way to live, a daily set of tasks designed to expand your life as a whole, taking you to all new heights and possibilities.

**POINT #4:** These possibilities are available to you. You just need to be awakened to these possibilities so you can grasp the belief of the man you will be and the life you will build.

**POINT #5:** All I am giving you is the chance to take on this system, as I have, and become someone you never thought possible. The decision is ultimately yours.

# 3

═══

# THE CHALLENGING EVOLUTION

*"Truth is stranger than fiction, but it is because Fiction is obliged to stick to possibilities; Truth isn't."*
**- Mark Twain**

Have you ever thought about what it means to be a man? Do you know what it takes to be a man? Or what you are supposed to be doing as a man in this modern world?

To start looking for the answers, we must go back to the time before the industrial revolution. A few centuries ago, in the late 1800s, this was not even a question. If you were a male, you were a man raised by men. There was no confusion about the meaning of a man, and masculinity was a trait shown to boys at a young age.

For most of society in these times, the way of living occurred with Dad, Mum, and children co-creating life together. The masculine and feminine energies were clear, and they were seen distinctly within the roles of the household. The man being the head of the house. The Dad would typically wake up early in the morning and head out to work on the farm. There was no big commute to work as the farm was the centre of the community. There was someone else who went to work with Dad, watching and helping him work every day. That person was little Billy.

Little Billy would go to work with his Dad and be by his side every single day. Little Billy would see what life was like as a man and how being a man worked. From breakfast to lunch to dinner, little Billy had a role model to look up to. Being educated taught respect, hard work, responsibility, and the connection with family. EVERY... SINGLE... DAY. Dad was demonstrating to his son the answer to our question,

**'How Do I Be A Man?'**

What came next was the Industrial Revolution, which caused a massive shift in the mindset and evolution of men. With this change came promise and opportunity: more money, more jobs, and a life closer to the city. Although men going to work at this time had to make a sacrifice, it was a sacrifice most of them were willing to pay. This sacrifice brought with it a whole series of new problems that nobody could have foreseen.

This promise and opportunity allowed families to move into the city from the farms, not needing to worry about bad weather or a starving family due to crops having a bad season and the backbreaking work that came with farming. All they had to do was leave during the day and head for the factory or office.

For the first time in recorded history, men were required to leave home early and travel a long way to work.[5] A place where little Billy

THE MODERN MAN'S CODE TO MANHOOD | 19

was not allowed to be side by side, working and learning from his male role model, his Dad. But this was only the start of the de-evolution for men. The fathers would return home late, tired and exhausted from the daily grind. Falling quickly to sleep that evening and only to wake up the following morning to do it all over again. On the odd occasion that Billy had not yet gone to sleep, the attempts by his father to fulfil his role were average at best, given his exhausted state. For all the time that he was away from the family, Mum had to take on being both the mother and father. This meant that Billy was not learning from a man how to be a man.

That's not all: back on the farm, men were required to solve problems using their initiative and creativity. Always finding better ways to do things, becoming more efficient and better equipped. These traits were drilled out of a man in the industrial age, as he would have been punished for innovation and creativity. There was a system within these factories to be followed and not be disrupted or changed, which is still current in workplaces today.

Men were essentially becoming just another cog in the machine or system – going to work to bring home the money. If a step was taken outside of this system or machine, a replacement was brought in, shifting the mindset to men becoming a disposable tool. This shift brought the belief that all a man does is go to work, do what he is told, make some money, provide for his family, come home and do it all again the next day, not actually needing to or even encouraged to think anymore.

At the time, though, it was not seen like this; fathers and men looked at this in a positive light. The family had more money whilst Mum and the kids could experience more in the city. They now had better clothes, bigger houses, and more food. It seemed as though everything was working out.

This might only seem like a small shift in the journey and hardly a big deal. Although when you think about a plane travelling only by coordinates, a shift by just one degree will change the direction entirely off-course over time. This small shift in an aircraft could miss the destination by 1km when flying only 50kms. This slight shift in direction can be the difference that forced a few generations to shift years of fatherhood.

To further solidify this mindset of men being away from their families and becoming a disposable tool, the World Wars occurred. Men were required to join the Army/Military to protect their countries. In doing this, men again felt the guidance and force of becoming just another cog in the system. The Army has no place for feelings or emotions. Feelings and expressing emotion will get you killed, resulting in death for you and other members of your squad. These emotions will also get in the way when the time comes if you are required to kill another man. So, the belief was made that 'feeling' must be suppressed, silenced, sedated and shut off completely.

While these men were off fighting for their countries, the mothers were left on their own to run the household and look after the children. This led to the need for women to enter the workforce and take over the jobs in the factories just to be able to afford to put food on the table. I take my hat off to these women, as it must have been a long hard slog, having to take on both roles as the provider and carer, not knowing if or when the men in their life would return.

A boy growing up in this time would have witnessed his father either off at war, working tirelessly to provide for the family, or maybe even both. The Army taught a whole generation of men how to not show emotion and suppress all feelings; they were taught not to feel. Think about the extent of the training that is now required to get into one of the armed forces. The brutal restrictions of sleep, the conditions needed to be endured and the barking of orders coming for the leaders. No wonder why men stopped feeling... It wasn't the Army's fault; this was required at the time.

All this led to women being pushed into needing to take on both parenting roles. They had to try to teach boys to be men because their fathers were too busy trying to be the breadwinners or off at war.

So, boys like Billy saw a distorted version of what it meant to be a man: to go out and make money and get stuff done regardless of how you feel. Do not whine about it, do not talk about it, and do not even think about getting emotional about it. Shut up, don't feel anything, just go make money to provide for the family. Then come home and be too exhausted to give any attention to his wife or kids.

This can be seen clearly when older men are on their death beds after a whole life of being silenced, suppressed, and sedated. Knowing their time here on earth is almost over, they recognise that this is the time to finally reach out to their sons, brothers, and fathers, finally telling them how they genuinely feel. They say, 'I love you.' Maybe even for the first time. It takes being on their deathbed to open up and express their feelings.

### 'I Haven't Even Finished Yet!'

At some point between the 1960s and 1990s, feminism started to take a distorted trajectory. Feminists shifted from wanting to have a voice and be equal (which are all great things, don't get me wrong) to taking on a twisted narrative in which they are the same as men and no longer require them.

Men and women will never be the same. Equal, yes. They can be equal, but they will never be the same. A penis and a vagina can and will never be the same. There are women, and there are men. It also doesn't matter what your sexual orientation is. They are not the same, and none is superior to any other!

With this new-aged feminism, men now have to battle the masculine energy from females too. No longer is the man's role simply to go to work and bring home the money. Women can make their own money, support themselves, and be the provider. All this leads men to even greater confusion over the question:

### 'How Do I Be A Man Now?'

The idea of simply working hard to provide for the family is now gone. Men are being told they need to be the man, but nobody can tell or teach us what it even means to be a man. We are unsure if we can even talk to anyone because we keep hearing that showing emotion is weak and for pussies. So how do we answer this question of what being a man is? Is anyone out there that can teach us this?

To add yet another obstruction to this situation, along comes what is known as the information age. With everything so easily available on-line, only one click away, there is absolutely no incentive to become a man. A guy could be in his 40s and still live like a guy in his 20s: working a boring 9-5, playing video games, watching Netflix late at night, staying up drinking with his mates, using apps like tinder to get laid by girls as much as 10 to 20 years younger than him with minimal effort. And if all that doesn't work out, there's always a shit ton of free and High-Definition porn just one click away. Over 35% of male internet usage is men watching porn or of that nature.[6] Tell me that's not an issue in itself! It doesn't do anything but fill your mind with a fake reality. Unfortunately, for many men, myself included, porn was where we first learn about sex.

### 'What Incentive Does A Guy Or A Boy Get These Days For Actually Becoming A Man?'

Today, you don't have to look too far to see we have the growing issues of what psychiatrists call 'extended adolescents'.[7] Boys are remaining boys into their 30s and 40s, refusing to grow up. Why would a guy want to grow up? Divorce rates are at their highest, and nobody is staying married. Broken families are everywhere. Social media is not helping them to be a man, reality TV isn't encouraging any guys to be men, and YouTube certainly isn't teaching us. There are more single mothers than ever before.

So, we end up in the place, looking at all this pain, frustration, and confusion, only to come up with yet another question: WHY?

### 'Why Be A Man?'

As we fast forward to today, modern men or boys have become lost, confused, weakened, suppressed, and all masculinity has been drained from inside them. Hiding behind their career, hiding behind excuses of a bad upbringing, or just being 'too busy' so they don't have to confront the truth of who they are or what they want from their lives. They are becoming incapable of actual human interaction, incapable of discovering what masculinity is, incapable of taking responsibility for their lives, and left feeling guilty if any sort of masculinity is found. School is beating the masculinity out of a boy from the first day he walks on the grounds. There is no guidance, no role models, no help, and no programs for guys. So, they end up in a place without a clue of what being a man is or whether there is even such a thing anymore. It's not their fault; it's not their fathers' or grandfathers' fault. It is just a fact of the reality from the past that resulted in men experiencing a devolution of what it is to be a man over time.

These lost men often isolate themselves from other men, stating that they are independent and self-reliant. Although, in reality, they are hiding, they are disconnected and confused. Believing that having real connections with other men is a sign of weakness and labelled as being a pussy.

Being a man is often related to how successful one is, the size of his bank account, the amount of women or good looks of the woman hanging off his arm, what car he drives, what house he lives in, or the size of his biceps. Mastering one or two of these areas doesn't make you a man.

### 'There is Still Hope!'

You must embrace and reconnect the different parts of masculinity that have been lost or seem out of reach. We do this by marrying together and developing all modern masculinity components, what it takes to be a man and a modern-day king. It is not just one or two aspects. To do this, you must become a master of your physical self, financial self, relationship/romantic self, and spiritual self as a man and within your spiritual mind. This starts with changing your relationship with yourself.

Unfortunately, there is no paved path to being a man or discovering your masculinity. It's a path you must carve and forge for yourself, both on your own and by banding together with other men, which is the foundation of why the AMD brotherhood was built. A band of brothers and men who are like you and living by the same Code. They're no better than you, myself included. We are just further down this path. It's not a race, nor is it a competition between any other man. We are all in this together, arm in arm. The only competition is yourself. To be better than you were yesterday.

### Un-Reality Becoming Reality

It's becoming more and more obvious that we as men have a real hard time facing the facts and facing our reality. We are becoming so filtered as men that we cannot see or even tell what is real or what is fake anymore. Stuck in this place, which sometimes seems real, and it can seem so much better here than the twisted reality of what is actually going on inside our lives. So, we believe, 'I think I'll stay in this un-real but real place.' Using anything to escape the reality of real life.

Not just men, but women too, have become so used to lying, pretending, covering up, and living in this fake reality, that the average person can't take a simple photo and post it on Instagram without filtering it first.

Reality TV was first built to get some insight into people's lives in the raw and on a level that they were 100% real. But now, it's no less scripted than any other sitcom or movie out there.

Facebook, Instagram, and other social media platforms were built to be a place for people to share who they are and have the chance to stay connected easier through media. Now, hundreds of thousands of software developers on these platforms have given us, the users, an option to filter the shit out of everything and leave this place just as fake.

To show even more than men struggle with the facts, let's talk about going to the doctors. Many men don't want to go for a check-up because they know they have been neglecting their bodies and aren't treating themselves as they need to be. They would rather just ignore the situation than go out and find the facts. Thinking, 'What I don't know won't hurt me; it will go away if I ignore it.'

If you cannot deal with the facts of your own life, you can't deal with reality, and if you cannot deal with reality, you will never be able to create new possibilities for yourself.

We would rather pull the blinds over the situation and just pretend everything is great from the outside, acting as though life is perfect by posting something on social media to further cement this fake reality. 'Look how great my life is!' We know it's not like that deep down, so we escape at any chance we get.

For a few years, I was exactly the same. People looking in from the outside thought my life was great. I was making good money, always travelling, and living a great life, but little did anyone know my life was imploding on the inside. I couldn't handle the reality, I couldn't face the facts, and I hated my life. This led me down a heavy suppression of excessive workouts, alcohol, drugs, porn, movies, anything and everything I could do to mask and cover up what was really happening. That led me to become trapped in a self-imposed deep pit of sorrow and having to face some dark, dark shit.

This is me being real, and this is me being raw, me being vulnerable, and this is me being honest. Are you prepared to get this real? Are you prepared to get this raw and honest? You will never be able to unlock new possibilities if you cannot face the facts. You will never be able to reach new heights if you continue to accept your current reality the way it is without beginning to question it.

How do you get to this level? How do you get this real, raw, and honest?

The answer is through a combination of the MMC, the Daily 8, and the tools accompanying this system. This brotherhood supports you. One of these tools is known as The Flips, which we will cover in Chapter 10. A tool of discovery and realisation that you can use to allow you to get real and discover the truth in every situation. Designed to get you out of the stories and lies you are telling, taking you to a place of clarity, calm, and focus. When you adopt this way of life, your life will reach all-new heights at a dramatic pace.

When you try to change reality, you are going against everything that is.

## KEY POINTS

**POINT #1:** The Industrial Revolution caused a massive shift in the mindset and evolution of men.

**POINT #2:** For the first time in recorded history, men were required to leave home early and travel a long way to work.

**POINT #3:** Men were essentially becoming just another cog in the machine or system – going to work to bring home the money.

**POINT #4:** The World Wars meant men were required to join the Army/Military.

**POINT #5:** The Army has no place for feelings or emotions, so the belief was made that 'feeling' must be suppressed, silenced, sedated and shut off completely.

**POINT #6:** All this led to women being pushed into needing to take on both parenting roles.

**POINT #7:** They had to try to teach boys to be men because their fathers were too busy trying to be the breadwinners or off at war.

**POINT #8:** Between the 1960s and 1990s, feminism started to take a distorted trajectory.

**POINT #9:** Feminists shifted from wanting to have a voice and be equal, to taking on a twisted narrative in which they are the same as men and no longer require them.

**POINT #10:** You must embrace and reconnect the different parts of masculinity by marrying together and developing all modern masculinity components, what it takes to be a man and a modern-day king.

**POINT #11:** You will never be able to reach new heights if you continue to accept your current reality the way it is without beginning to question it.

# 4

## THE FATHER & YOU

*'Many men go to their graves convinced
that they have been an inadequate
human being.'*
**- Iron John**

I ask this question to most of the men I work with; 'would you be relieved if your father died tomorrow?' I would say about 80% of them would say yes. If that alone isn't alarming, I don't know what is. Even worse, 90% of my clients have said their fathers would fit into at least one of the following; he was non-existent or never home, he abused him or his family, they hated each other, or he was way too hard/strict. Yes, that's 90%.

Before we go any further into this chapter, I want to give you a full disclosure. At the time of writing, I'm not a father myself. You can take that and think, 'well I'm not listening to this guy,' or you can humble yourself and just hear me out throughout this chapter. I've worked with hundreds of men through hundreds of different situations to know enough about this. As we go through this chapter, you'll soon be able to tell.

I firmly believe that the father is the most influential parent to the child. Don't get me wrong, the role the mum plays is irreplaceable, absolutely necessary, and cannot be done by the man. But 99% of the time, the mother's love is always there, and her attention is never far away.[8] The father, on the other hand, is completely different. A boy looks up to his father to see what a man is supposed to be like, and a girl looks up to him to see what she needs in a potential partner. If you don't consciously give your children a role model to look up to, they will find one, and sometimes that can be the local drug dealer or 'bad boy'.

## Fathers & Self-Confidence

Let me give you an example. A previous client of mine had a father who was strict with him from a young age. He was pushing him so hard to make it to the NRL and would take him to every training, be there at every game and never miss any chance to make his son play. Where the problem started to come in was how critical his dad was over every tiny little thing. Listening to this man speak, I could already begin to tell what was going on for him. He would say how great he felt after coming off the field playing a really great game, only to reach his father, who pointed out the smallest mistake and focused on that. This started from his first game when he was 6, all the way to his last at 21.

Imagine this; you're an eight-year-old boy who just thought you'd play one of your best games. Your father doesn't give you any praise and tells you all about the small errors you made. How do you think your self-esteem would develop after 15 years of this?

As you could have guessed, my client had major self-worth, self-esteem and confidence issues. It wasn't until we got to the bottom of this that he could then be liberated. His mother never wanted to come to the games and didn't like footy, but her not even being the slightest interested didn't affect his confidence. This supports my claim that the father is the most influential in the child's development.

I could write a hundred stories of the role fathers have played in the adult problems my clients have come to me with. But don't get me wrong; not all dads are negative or detrimental to their children's lives. And you reading this book means that you actively want to improve yourself, so I'd say you're at worse, a half-decent father. The benefits of this might really shock you. The picture is stunningly clear when you consider the following research. If there is a father in the home, then statistically, both boys and girls have higher self-esteem, they do better in school and stay in school longer, become better qualified and are more likely to be employed. They are less likely to have trouble with the law, they are less likely to be victims of assault, rape, or sexual abuse, or have problems with drugs and alcohol. Girls are less likely to experience early sexual intercourse or teen pregnancy, and boys are less likely to be violent or belong to a gang.[9]

You may have never got what you needed from your father, and he might not have been the best example of fatherhood. They don't teach this at schools, and you may have been trying to invent fatherhood from scratch, which is a difficult task. Many men resent their fathers for not being the 'dream father' they'd hoped for. You know, that father image we so desperately wanted our fathers to be, but more often than not, it was only a dream. I want you to understand that, as hard as this may be, it's not your father's fault. Going back to the previous chapter, fatherhood has been lost over the last few generations by no-ones fault. So your father was doing the best he could with his resources at the time. You may not see that, but you see the situation through your eyes, not his.

## Letting Go of The War With Your Masculinity

If you are at war with your father in your head and haven't been able to bring that to peace, that same war can be taken into a war with masculinity itself. Whether you like it or not, your masculinity is based on his. If you reject your father, you may be the complete opposite. If you looked up to him, you would have modelled him and are most like not far from the apple tree, as the saying goes. If he was absent, dead, ignored you, or always seemed too busy to spend time with you, his love and attention most likely were the things you craved the most. This leaves a hole waiting to be filled.

This hole can be attempted to be filled by others, but your father's place in your life will still be there. It doesn't matter if he was an alcoholic or drug addict, abused your mum or other children, died, or abandoned you; he still matters to you. He will haunt you from the inside until you come to terms with him.

It's common for men to want to avoid being anything like their fathers. They consciously try to be the complete opposite of him in as many ways as possible. This doesn't make you any freer from letting go of the internal war you have with him. If anything, it's making you just as trapped. If your father was a drinker, you might have never touched a drink in your life. If your father lives in the country, you might live in a big city. You might have followed the corporate role if your father was a tradesman. But this doesn't deal with the problem; it just pushes it to the side.

## Wound In Need Of Healing

There is a danger that you will not become fully mature if you can't reach a place where you can love and respect your father. And by that, I mean deep down, and not just saying it. There are many men whose fathers abandoned them or died at a young age. There are many men whose mothers restricted access to their fathers for whatever reason. Some might have even committed suicide.

If this happened while the boy was still young, it could lead to a lot of hurt, pain, confusion, and mixed messages. The young boy may think it was all his fault. 'What have I done to make my father leave?' 'Is there something wrong with me?' 'If he loved me, he wouldn't be gone.' This is the message all children take from abandonment, which needs to be healed.

We try to suppress this pain by working hard, living in denial and abusing substances. Although, this deepened pain can often develop into outbursts, which are masked by anger. In my experience, anger isn't the problem; there's an underlying unhealed deeper cause of this issue. Sadness, pain, hurt, neglect or abandonment can be examples of this. Unfortunately, this is seen as a man having anger issues, and he's often forced or chooses to go to anger management, counsellors or therapy to deal with this. The number of men I've worked with who have completed these programs and felt no better clearly indicates that something is not working and something else is a play here. Anger is the outcome, not the cause.

In my late teens and early twenties, I was very focused on the deficiencies of my father, blaming him for the traits or behaviours that I had pick-up from him and the things I didn't get from him as a young boy. Then, one evening, I was walking along the beach, watching the orange tinge from the sun shining across the waves. It was a peaceful evening, with barely anyone around.

My phone went off with a text message; I can't recall exactly what it was about or who it was from. Whatever it was, it gave me some memories of my father. Then the strangest thing happened; as I felt my eyes getting heavy, I started to cry. Suddenly, my mind started showing me all these times when my dad had been caring, loving and opposite to the image I'd had in my mind. Laying on the couch with him at night, keeping me warm at sporting games, holding me tight when I was scared of fireworks. I had blocked out all these memories because they didn't match the story I had formed in my mind. This came at the time when I was finally ready to stop blaming him, and my mind wanted to show me.

## Respect

Whether your father is around or not, coming to terms with him and having an understanding view of him is so important. If you don't, it will haunt you until you do. This is especially important if you are a father or you are in any type of leadership role in your career or business. When you can respect your dad and accept his model of the world, only then will others respect you. Respect is not what you think.

Your father (or father figure) is the first man you love, just like your mother is the first woman you love. They are the first people you 'let in.' If you feel like your father hasn't given you what you wanted or needed, more often than not, you won't respect him. When you don't respect, you cannot receive not only respect but love, care and other gifts they have to give you. Again, just reaffirming that you didn't get what you wanted. How can you get what you want if you're not open to receiving it?

Unconsciously, this lack of respect can be taken in your career, workplace and fatherhood of your own. If you think of what disrespect is, it's kind of like blindness and naivety. Essentially, blinding our vision – blinding our vision to what we want to see.

Don't get me wrong; not everyone deserves our respect. But there are always things in people that we can respect. The things that are good, despite the bad. You can't have good without bad.

## Awareness

Being more self-aware and understanding towards yourself is always the best strategy. Notice when your buttons are pushed, and be comfortable about why they get pushed. Life is one big lesson; your triggers are being shown for you to heal and grow. Be grateful and take advantage of these people who have shown you this.

For example, if your father was angry, aggressive, shouting or violent, notice when these buttons start to be pressed. Then have some compassion for yourself as you are just reacting in the way your father has taught you. Once you notice the first physical sign that you are about to lose your cool, what actions can you take? Can you excuse yourself and leave the room to calm down? Can you take 3 deep breaths or count to ten? Acting through emotion is never the best way to deal with a situation. It's ok to take a moment or two, think about what you want to do or say and then proceed.

## Fatherhood

Boys are so hungry for a male role model that they will look elsewhere if you don't provide it. If you don't consciously be their role model, your sons and daughters *will* find others to model; you might not like that outcome. This lack of role models shows up in everyone's life. The 50-year-old lady who's unconsciously sabotaged every relationship because she didn't get love from her father, so now she doesn't know how to handle it when received. The 12-year-old riding push bikes after dark in the shopping centre, disrespecting any rules or authority figures. His father left him, which has left the boy with a skewed perception of older men and a lack of respect for authority. 16-year-olds are taking their own lives because it is 'the easiest way out.' A role model, a guide or an ear to listen to could be the thing that saves these teenagers' lives.

If you are a father, this should be one of your #1 roles. Being a father is a commitment, a duty, and a responsibility, and you shouldn't run from it. Don't use the excuse of not having enough time. No amount of income or nothing you buy will outweigh the effects of a dad who isn't around enough. Today we have wimpish fathers everywhere. One would rather stay at work late till the kids go to bed, so they don't have to deal with it. They leave discipline to their wives or, even worse, undermine them. Blurting out things like 'just let them be – they're just being kids,' or 'calm down, it doesn't really matter.' These men are likely in for an early divorce and a terrible sex life!

When you, as the father, are doing your bit, you can allow your partner to step into and embrace her feminine. She can relax, feel supported, and step out of her mum role while stepping into being your partner/ lover. I will go into this in a lot more detail in the next chapter. It is not hard to spot a relationship where those women feel backed up by their husbands in the home. They are more relaxed, warm and feminine. If a woman has to do all the tough stuff, discipline and battle the kids, call the plumber and make the decisions, she looks hard, tired and run-down. She doesn't even need to say anything; you can just tell by her body language what she's thinking 'my husband is too weak.'

When you take a firm stand on what is and isn't acceptable, following up in a non-violent but firm manner enables your partner to relax and remain loving. However, this doesn't mean both partners must do everything; the responsibilities aren't one-sided. A father's discipline will not be effective unless he also plays a loving and involved role with his child.

A boy feels safe and can find his feet easier as an individual when he experiences his father's slightly stronger, slightly more conditional love. As a young man, he responds to women as equals because he sees himself as capable of standing alone without mothering. The likelihood of him wanting to be mothered will decrease, and both mothers and future partners will find this a great relief. A fully-grown man makes a much better partner.

---

## KEY POINTS

**POINT #1:** 'Would you be relieved if your father died tomorrow?'

**POINT #2:** A boy looks up to his father to see what a man is supposed to be like, and a girl looks up to him to see what she needs in a potential partner.

**POINT #3:** If you don't consciously give your children a role model to look up to, they will find one, and sometimes that can be the local drug dealer.

**POINT #4:** You may have never gotten what you needed from your father, and he might not have been the best example of fatherhood.

**POINT #5:** If you are at war with your father in your head and haven't been able to bring that to peace, that same war can be taken into a war with masculinity itself.

**POINT #6:** Whether your father is around or not, coming to terms with him and having an understanding view of him is so important. If you don't, it will haunt you until you do.

**POINT #7:** When you, as the father, are doing your bit, you can allow your partner to step into and embrace her feminine.

**POINT #8:** A fully-grown man makes a much better partner.

# 5

## THE MAN & THE WOMAN

*"If your emotional abilities aren't in hand, if you don't have self-awareness, if you are not able to manage your distressing emotions, if you can't have empathy and have effective relationships, then no matter how smart you are, you are not going to get very far."*
## - Daniel Goleman

It was the end of 2015, a few months after I'd decided to embark on this journey of fixing myself. This was when google became my best friend as I looked up everything I could, trying to find that one piece of information that would make a big difference in my life. Suddenly, I thought I had found the resources to help fix my confidence. I can remember thinking at the time, 'have I found what I've wanted since high school already... surely this can't be that easy?'

Unfortunately, it was nowhere near being that easy. At that time, I was still right into pursuing health and fitness as a career, and I had email subscriptions and newsletters coming from people all around the world. At one stage, I was getting over 100 emails a day from 100 different people. It was nearly a full-time job going through all the information daily, and I loved it. It was different back then; emails seemed longer and much more information-based.

One of the guys I followed at the time was a real hard man, and I admired how confident he was. I looked up to him, mainly because I desperately wanted to have confidence as high as his. Every day, I would scroll through my long list of emails to find his, and it would always be the first one I read. One of these emails caught my attention. The headline wrote 'my son now has confidence'. It caught my attention so much that I still remember it today.

He spoke about a counsellor named Chris and how he helped his son who was struggling socially. As I read the email, it was a spitting image of my life, almost perfectly. That was it; if he can help his son, he can help me! So I clicked on the link, but nothing happened. The link was broken. I went from high excitement to utter disappointment within a few seconds. I replied to his email every day for a week with no reply until I eventually gave up.

A few weeks later, I was reading another email from one of the other 99 emails in my inbox. They were talking about a guy who helped men with confidence so they could attract and meet women. This got my attention again. Then I saw it; his name was Chris. I couldn't believe it. I clicked the link, bought his few hundred dollar program, and was on top of the world. Unfortunately, I just assumed it was the same Chris, soon to find out it definitely wasn't. What I actually bought was a series of videos teaching men how to approach women in broad daylight – sober! It was way out of my capabilities at that time.

Included in that course were 5 interviews with different women asking them what they love about men and what they want in a relationship. I briefly watched them at the time, but that's as far as I got. It wasn't until a year or two ago that I somehow found the login and passwords and re-watched them. Wow, with my level of awareness now, this was a totally different experience.

### If You Change, The World Around You Changes

Here's the thing, these interviews were still the exact same, with the exact same 5 women, and nobody had changed anything about them. Why did they change so much? Because I had changed. This is a massive misconception and issue I commonly hear, 'my partner has changed,' 'she's not the same as when we first got together,' or 'we never have fun anymore'. We think things should stay the same from the first time we meet and start dating. The reality is that we are constantly changing, and you need to grow and continuously work on the relationship. So if you begin to work on yourself and improve, as you are by going through this book, the people around you, including your partner, will change. Not because of them, but because of you. If you change, the world around you changes, including your relationship, for better or worse.

I learned so much from those 5 interviews about women; hearing things from their perspective was amazing. I could relate to their words and directly correlate them to what my male clients were thinking and experiencing. More importantly, I learnt more about men and how to help us navigate women. Since then, I've helped men on the brink of divorce to save their marriages. I've helped men reconnect with their kids after not speaking in years. There's been men who have been single for most of their own life; within weeks, they have found their dream partners. I want you to learn about women and relationships in this chapter so you can show up for them at your best. Eradicate the thinking that 'women are complicated,' and you'd never be able to understand them. That's bullshit; if that's your thinking, then you're just too lazy to put in the effort. First, before you can even begin to understand anyone else, you need to understand yourself and how to play out your role in a relationship.

## Women Want Men Who Are Real

As discussed in previous chapters, we've gone through a few phases of manhood. Before the industrial revolution and world wars, men were real, men were strong, men were loving, and they were 'around'. In the second phase, around the first half of the twentieth century, men were often more commonly emotionally 'switched off'. Not knowing how to show emotion, and their wives found them difficult to know or deal with. Here, the expectations seemed so high that many men simply fell into the suppression trap. Starting and ingraining the thought of being a 6 pack deep helped them to 'cope' with their partners.

In the third phase, the last 20-30 years, men have begun to have more heart, and it was ok to be shown. Things like love, affection and compassion for their wives and children, grief, concern and sadness didn't have to be hidden away, and these men could talk. These new men were someone you could talk to; they were more real.

However, in more recent years, it's failed to level out. Men have become weaker, and we don't want weaker men. We need men with emotional intelligence who can shift gears when needed. Firstly, a woman wants to know that she can walk down the street with her man; if a situation arises, she knows he is capable of handling anything and protecting her. Secondly, she wants to know that 5 minutes later, they can sit on the couch and connect on a deeper level. That's a man with emotional intelligence; that's a man who can shift gears when required. On the other hand, a man guided by his feelings wouldn't be able to let that go and would most likely be still wound up an hour later.

## The 'Sensitive New Age Guy'

The rise of the 'sensitive New Age guy' has begun due to the massive mixed messages from everywhere. Boys raised by single mothers, spending their time at home with mostly females, getting taught in schools by 80% female teachers and the 'pedestaling women pandemic', to name a few, have all contributed to this. The 'sensitive New Age guy' is not someone you would look to if a car broke down, if a house was on fire, if someone was breaking into your house or even during hard times in a marriage. These men put women on a pedestal and then resent them for being there.

## Fortitude & Heart

How do we counteract this and build ourselves into a well-rounded man? How do we begin the revolution of Phase 4, the mentally strong, emotionally intelligent awake man? By combining fortitude from Phase 1 and heart from Phase 3. This is an Advanced Man.

Fortitude is the ability to stand firm, endure and be true to your word. Not take the easy road, not listen to the little voice we all have inside of us and don't hide from things you don't feel like doing. A man with fortitude is mentally strong and someone you can count on. Depending on the situation and for the right reasons, he would be willing to sacrifice his life for the people he cares about.

When a man has mental fortitude and heart, a woman can be his partner, not his mother. Women have the unhealthy tendency to take care of the men in their lives and then resent them, just like men put women on a pedestal and then resent them for being there. The truth is that women were made to nurture, but in healthy relationships, this nurturing must be done in a give-and-take context. They want to serve, yet they also need to be served. They want to give, but they also need to feel that they're receiving. They want to be able to take care of their man, but just as much, they want to feel that he's taking good care of them. Here's one way that might help.

### The 5 Love Languages™

A few years ago, my audiobook subscription was my biggest learning tool. Each month I'd see where I was in my life and pick a book to suit my current situation. At the time, I'd just entered into a new relationship. So as the theme continued, I searched for books about sex and relationships. There were some extremely informative and eye-opening books, and I learned a lot. Even better, I could implement it straight away. Information is basically useless without action or implementation.

One of those was *The 5 Love Languages*™ by Gary Chapman.[10] If you've never heard of this book, this will change the way you view relationships. Gary speaks about the 5 different needs of people he's noticed over his lifetime as a counsellor. The 5 languages are 1. Words of Affirmation, 2. Acts of Service, 3. Receiving Gifts, 4. Quality Time and 5. Physical Touch. He has a free The Love Language™ Quiz[11] and I highly recommend you sit down and find out what you and your partners' love languages are. Then commit to meeting that need. This is how you can keep your relationship in healthy polarity between give-and-take.

### Answers or Support?

It is a masculine trait to always want to fix or find solutions. The masculine grows by challenge, but the feminine grows by praise[12]. Understanding this can save you a lot of arguments and potential disconnect. She wants to feel heard, loved and supported, and you cannot do this if you're giving her a solution to her problem. To become a better communicator, you must become a better listener. This is even more important when it comes to your partner.

This may be hard at first if you're so used to being the problem solver but fail to pick up on her cues. As soon as you begin to notice yourself wanting to give advice, ask her, 'do you want support or answers?' Most times, she doesn't want answers; she wants ears. Not only will you begin to understand her and pick up on the cues, you're also showing her that you care. Now, if you can't put up with her talking, or you think she's bitching, you need to question why you're even in that relationship in the first place. Are you taking the easy road?

90% of a woman's emotional problems stem from feeling unloved[13], which is exactly why she doesn't want answers. Don't stand back, analyse her and give her a diagnosis (aka your opinion) like you're a therapist. Give her your love; show her that you care. Look deeply into her eyes, hold her, smile, and just listen. Chances are, her emotional problem will dissolve. This doesn't necessarily fix the situation; she may still need to deal with it. You now may be in a position to be able to help her with that if she wants your help. Either way, the emotional aspect will be transformed to love.

## Neediness

If a man wants a woman who doesn't want him, he cannot win her over, no matter how hard he tries. His neediness will damage any possible relationship. He will lose trust and come across as desperate. As soon as she feels his neediness, he needs her more than she needs him, or she can feel the desperation, she'll lose any attraction to him. This is something I have to remind 80% of my clients that are going through a separation or divorce. Don't be needy, don't be clingy and don't be desperate. If your partner is the most important thing in your life, it will rock your world if anything happens to her or she breaks it off.

I look back on my teenage relationship ending when I was 19 or 20. We had only been together for about a year or two before she broke up with me, and it rocked me for months. I'd never experienced anything like it before. For the next 3 months, I spent my time trying to weasel my way back into her life. I would drive past her work with loud music, hoping she'd see me. I tried to hang out with her sister more, so I could be around. It's quite pathetic when I think about it now, but it just shows that being that needy puppy trying to win her back will never work.

## Purpose

People are attracted to others who are driven and have their 'life on track.' They are ambitious, motivated, hard-working and committed, and most perceive these as attractive traits. When a man has a purpose and knows where he wants to go, others want to be around him. They want to feed off him and also help push him. The same is true for your partner.

Many men who joined my 1on1 programs have told me about their partners' concerns halfway through the program. Whether it be due to insecurities or a just general concern, these women were worried about their partners leaving them and outgrowing them. They could see the changes, the progress and the higher sense of purpose, which worried them. All it took was a conversation between them, and the worry dissipated, but what happened next is interesting. 90%, if not all of them, saw huge improvements in their relationships and sex lives. This is what happens when you are living true to your purpose. Now you might be in a position where you have no idea what your purpose is. Good! We will cover that in a later chapter.

A woman doesn't really want to be her man's number one, and she might seem to want to be the most important thing in his life. However, if she is the most important thing, obviously his purpose is not. When she feels her man has made her number one, she'll pick up that he's not fully dedicated or directed to his growth. Purpose and neediness go hand in hand. When she becomes a man's highest priority, he'll find his happiness becomes dependent on her. This will make her feel overwhelmed by his neediness.

Your woman really wants you to be totally dedicated to your highest purpose, but also to love her fully. Although she would never admit it, she wants to feel that her man would be willing to sacrifice their relationship for the sake of his highest purpose. This is more commonly seen with men in the armed forces leaving their partners as they go away on missions.

## Balance

Don't get me wrong; I'm not saying you must spend all your time working on or towards your purpose and disregarding your partner. This will be a balancing act that you will need to figure out for yourself. I can't tell you this, and she can't either, but you will be slowly able to pick up on her cues and how your relationship is tracking by looking at the facts. As David Deida explains in *The Way of The Superior Man*, 'your woman will be more fulfilled with 30 minutes a day of undivided attention and ravishing love than with a few hours of your weak and divided presence when your heart really isn't into it.'[14]

The time you spend with your partner should be the time you really want to be with her. If you are present with her and don't get distracted, I can guarantee your relationship will change from this one thing, stay present. Being present is so important that I've dedicated a whole chapter to it later in this book. During this present time you are spending with her, it's perfect timing to fill up her love bucket with her love language. Let me be clear with this. If you'd rather be doing something else, she'll feel it, and you will be dissatisfied.

In closing this chapter, I want to finish with one final question for you, and be real here: how committed are you to your current partner and relationship? If it's not 100%, I recommend you ask yourself some of the hard questions as to why it's not 100%. Cause nothing you do from this chapter will make a difference if you're not 100% into it. What would an Advanced Man do in this situation?

## KEY POINTS

**POINT #1:** When you change, the world around you changes

**POINT #2:** The reality is that we are constantly changing, and you need to grow and continuously work on the relationship.

**POINT #3:** A man with emotional intelligence is a man who can shift gears when required. A man guided by his feelings wouldn't be able to let go of events and situations for hours or even days.

**POINT #4:** Fortitude is the ability to stand firm, endure and be true to your word. A man with fortitude is mentally strong and someone you can count on.

**POINT #5:** When a man has mental fortitude and heart, a woman can be his partner, not his mother.

**POINT #6:** As soon as you begin to notice yourself wanting to give advice, ask her, 'do you want support or answers?' Most times, she doesn't want answers; she wants ears.

**POINT #7:** If a man wants a woman who doesn't want him, he cannot win her over, no matter how hard he tries. His neediness will damage any possible relationship.

**POINT #8:** How committed are you to your current partner and relationship? If it's not 100%, I recommend you ask yourself some of the hard questions as to why it's not 100%.

# 6

## THE PATH

*"No one saves us but ourselves. No one can and no one may. We ourselves must walk the path."*
**- Buddha**

There's a misconception in our modern society that we must have a path we need to take, and it must be decided before we even leave school. How is a boy, or anyone for that matter, expected to know exactly where they want to go in their life at the age of 16? It doesn't matter what school it is or even the country. We are being forced to make a big life decision in the direction we want to go in our lives after graduating from high school.

I understand why this decision needs to be made as university and college are just around the corner, and to be accepted into one of these facilities, the decision must be made a few years out. That is why so many of us, myself included, get to the age of 30 and have lost interest in where we are going and feel stuck with our current careers. That's if we chose a career in the first place and haven't just gone to do a 'useful' or 'bridging' subject at university or college to give us more time to find our path. Again, only to end up at the age of 30 with a few, for the most part, useless degrees and still no idea of where we want to go or what to do.

When I first started high school, I wanted to be a PE teacher; I thought it would be the best job ever. I was an outdoorsy and sporty kid who loved all forms of sport, so it seemed like the perfect fit. Until the end of grade 10, we had a few planning sessions on what subjects to choose for the last two years of school.

There was a tool online that allowed you to enter the possible job you wanted, and it would spit out the subjects to consider to reach that career target. So, I typed in PE teacher, and a bunch of subjects came up. The one that comes straight to mind is biology. It was a subject that everyone talked about being a challenging subject, and the teacher at my high school who taught biology happened to be one of the grumpiest old ladies I'd ever met in my life. However, I did what most 10th graders did; I followed that online tool and added biology to my subject list.

Half of my first year went by, and after failing biology up until that point, I thought, 'Fuck this subject and fuck being a PE teacher!'. I believed that I needed to succeed, and because I'd failed, I now needed a new path. That new 'path' came in the form of a carpentry apprenticeship.

By age 25, I had started asking and questioning whether I wanted to be doing this for the rest of my life. As most men do, I felt trapped in this industry where the money was good. However, a few years later, I took that leap and started to help other men in their lives, a pursuit that has grown into the AMD.

Becoming a human behaviour expert and life strategist was never something I had planned on doing or even thought about. I mean, I was struggling with so much of my own shit that all of my focus was directed to trying to get myself out of the hole I was stuck in. I couldn't imagine pulling other men out from the holes they were digging themselves when I was still in my own.

In my 8 years of searching, the path was always there for me; I just wasn't aware of it. Going from being asleep to awakened is another one of men's biggest challenges. Of course, being asleep means that men aren't even aware that this act of awakening and the challenges involved even exist.

I was asleep to the enjoyment I had when I helped grade 1s learn to swim. I was asleep to the problems of the guy on the bus who continually looked sad, even though all I wanted to do was go and talk to him. I was asleep to the fact that I found a sense of purpose in helping people. I was asleep to all these situations until I was awakened and could assess my life from this new perspective.

Creating the life you want is one of the hardest things you will do.

To understand where and how to create the life you want, first you need to find out where you currently are and where you want to be. There will be no journey without an exact starting point and endpoint in mind.

### Finding Your GPS

Imagine if you were travelling to a new destination and needed to use a GPS. Once you find where you want to go gives you a clear path to take and even redirects you back on track if you make a wrong turn. In that same situation, it's virtually useless if the GPS doesn't know where the starting point is. The same goes if there's a starting point but no destination of where to go to; again, it's useless.

Something I see in men every single day is that many of them walk around with no idea where they are going, no path to follow, no purpose to pursue, and no targets set. Again, the biggest problem here is that there is nobody to teach us and give us the guiding support that we need to find our path or even a guiding hand to push us in the right direction. For some of us, our path is predetermined by our parents and their beliefs of what we should be and who we should become, rather than our own.

## Concept #1

I want to introduce you to something called 'WTD': Walk... Think... Discover. Doing this allows the voice inside of you to finally speak in a way that you must listen to and, in turn, discover. This concept is simple, and it's one of the first and biggest exposures you will become awakened to when you start to do this type of inner work.

## Walk

At sunrise (this must be done at sunrise!), you will set a timer for 20 mins and just walk. No music, no phone calls, no headphones, no social media, absolutely nothing but yourself and your thoughts. It doesn't matter where you are walking or even in what direction. Just get up, get outside, pick a direction and start walking.

## Think

During your silent walk, you will be thinking and asking yourself two questions and two questions only: 'Where am I now?' and 'Who am I?'. For the whole 20 minutes while walking, you'll be going back and forth between those two questions. If you find your mind drifting off, then you come back to these questions. Think of them as an anchor that pulls you back when you start to drift off.

## Discover

Once the 20 minutes is up, your alarm will sound, at which point you will stop immediately. Find somewhere to sit and open your mobile phone to the voice recorder and record yourself answering those two questions you have been asking yourself for the last 20 minutes. This should only take about 5 minutes. Don't hold back on anything. The learnings and self-discoveries don't have to be positive or negative or anything else we might think they are. All we are doing is getting them out of our heads and on record without judgement.

When they are out of your head, your mind now won't be able to mess with them. Most people don't understand the power of just getting this out of their minds. If you don't, overwhelm will become a daily occurrence for you.

## Discovery

There is a second part to the 'discovery' phase. On the walk back, you will listen to your recording on repeat all the way back (you can use headphones here). Listening to your learnings and insights, through your own voice, and discovering where it is you are actually starting from.

This place of expanded awareness now makes up the starting location for your GPS. Finally, and maybe for the first time, you will have a clear picture of who you really are.

As discussed previously, a GPS is useless without a destination, which is why we add a second tool to discover your path.

This next tool is similar to the one used previously in finding your starting point, except the questions change. Exactly one week later, and at sunrise, you will get up again and walk. This time, your two questions will be, 'who do I want to become?' and 'where do I want to go?'. After 20 minutes, stop, record yourself, and listen on repeat all the way back.

After just one week, by listening to the voice inside of you, you start to become slightly awakened and consciously discover who you are and where you want to be. Possibly for the first time ever in your life, you now have the exact starting point and the exact destination of your GPS.

### 'Your Why'

The final tool I want to introduce you to for even more clarity around your 'why' or your 'purpose' is The Seven Layers Below Tool. This is a simple framework that many different people use, and I have often used it in my own life. It is the tool that brings up emotion in me every single time I do it. I want to show you an example of one I completed a few years prior. Not only so that you can see how it works but to show you that I am no different to any of you; I'm just a few years further down the path.

### Concept #2

It starts with the question, 'Why is it important for you to step into YOUR king and be the best man you can be?'

**Layer #1** – Stepping into my king and being the best man that I can be is important to me because:

*'I'm sick of living my life being stuck in 'this internal prison.' I'm always working, I haven't gotten anywhere in the last few years, and I want to live my life on my terms and with the freedom I desire.'*

**Layer #2** – *'Not being stuck in 'this internal prison,' living my life on my terms and with the freedom I desire.'*

Is important to me because:

*'I want to be in control of my life and not get pushed around by others. I now know there is so much more out there for me, and I feel like I'm wasting my value by just doing the same old thing'.*

**Layer #3 –** *'Being in control of my life, not getting pushed around by others and not wasting my value.'*

Is important to me because:

*'I want to leave a legacy, not only for my family and my kids but for my grandchildren and great-grandchildren. I don't want just to be just a father and a husband; I want to be their best friend and companion. I want to have a connection with them that I never had.'*

**Layer #4 –** *'Leaving a legacy and having a deeper connection than just that of a father and husband.'*

Is important to me because:

*'I don't want my future kids to grow up without that, and I know that the key to bringing my family together in this way starts with me. I have the power to create this for them and for me'.*

**Layer #5 –** *'I don't want my kids to grow up without that and knowing I have the power to create this.'*

Is important to me because:

*'it's something that I feel I didn't get as a boy in my life, and it's given me a higher purpose than just myself. Being able to help other men in their life also allows for massive growth in my personal life.'*

**Layer #6** – '*Being able to help other men in their lives while allowing massive growth in my own life.*'

Is important to me because:

'*I know how it feels, and I know that I have the power to improve my relationships as well as thousands of men's relationships with their families, parents, children and more importantly themselves.*'

**Layer #7** – '*Improving my relationships as well as 1000s of men's relationships with their families, parents, children, and themselves.*'

Is important to me because:

'*I will learn how to be the best father and husband I can be and pass that on to all the men inside the AMD brotherhood, so we grow as one. Learn – teach – grow – learn – teach – grow – learn – teach – grow. I'm an Advanced Man, and I'm building my tribe of Advanced Men*'

As you can see, upon completing this, I've found my deeper reasons, purpose, and my 'why.' This tool will only dive as deep as you are willing to let it. Get real, get raw, and get honest with your reasons; don't suppress or hold anything back. You are the only person that will ever see this if that's what you choose. If you don't have a big enough reason for doing something, you will never do it.

Why is procrastination such a big thing? Because if something is not important to you, there is no way you will ever feel like doing anything remotely close to that thing. If you find yourself procrastinating about work or school, the first thing you do is add it to the top of the Seven Layers Below Tool. Ask yourself why it's important to you, and keep this conversation going until you find a big enough reason for you to keep on doing it. If you can't find a big enough reason, then stop doing it. There's nothing wrong with stopping something if it doesn't serve you at a higher level.

This level of exposure and inquiry into yourself will ultimately allow you to become comfortable with yourself and with who you need to become.

## KEY POINTS

**POINT #1:** Going from being asleep to being awakened is another one of men's biggest challenges. Being asleep means that men aren't even aware that this act of awakening and the challenges involved even exist.

**POINT #2:** Creating the life you want is one of the hardest things you will do.

**POINT #3:** Get real, get raw, and get honest with yourself and the tools; don't suppress or hold anything back.

**POINT #4:** If you don't have a big enough reason for doing something, you will never do it.

**POINT #5:** This level of exposure and inquiry into yourself will ultimately allow you to become comfortable with yourself and with who you need to become.

# 7

## THE PURPOSE

*"Efforts and courage are not enough
without purpose and direction."*
**- John F. Kennedy**

Given this modern world that we live in, when we begin a conversation around purpose, there are two specific hurdles that many of us get caught up on. One is the 'need' for having a purpose, and the second is that a purpose should be some big, world-changing resolution like solving 'world peace,' 'ending poverty,' or some extreme radical movement.

This concept around 'finding our life purpose' has been blown right out of proportion by so-called 'gurus' and life coaches with the idea that every man, and person for that matter, is born into this world for some higher purpose, and it's now our life long cosmic mission to find it. Like it's some big elusive thing that must be found to live a successful life.

But here's the reality: every one of us is having a human experience on this earth. We've been put here for some unknown amount of time, at least unknown to us. During our time here, we do things; some are important, some are not so important, and others are just a waste of time. Those important things are the ones that bring meaning and happiness to our lives.

## The Biggest Killer

The biggest killer of your happiness is allowing others to be in control of your happiness. What you expect others to have or should be doing, how your parents should have parented you, what the government should be doing, what your partner should have done, how your boss should treat you... I could go on forever. All of these are killing your happiness. There's no surprise why 3$^{rd}$ world countries are always the ones with the happiest people on the earth; there's no 'expectation' for them.

Now, I'm not saying for you to be cold towards everyone. Having others around you can add to your happiness, but they are not responsibly for it. Let me say that again; other people are not responsible for your happiness. Happiness comes from within; when your inner world is strong, nothing outside can affect you.

I know this chapter is about purpose, and I could have written a lot more here on happiness, but I thought it was important to mention that there. Be mindful of how your expectations of others and the role they should be playing are dictating your happiness.

## The 3 Outcomes

If a man continues along with his life, searching for that higher purpose, as discussed, there are a few things that will happen. 1. A man will fall into the constant cycle of searching but not finding. 2. He will think he's found his purpose until, somewhere along the line, the realisation comes when it's not something that truly brings enjoyment and a sense of fulfilment to his life anymore, aka midlife crisis, or 3. He gives up on that search with the belief that 'I don't need a purpose' or 'I wasn't born to have a purpose like others are' or 'I'm happy with the way I am, working a job and just getting by each day.' FYI, all of them are bullshit stories.

I was fluctuating between a one and a three for most of my early 20s, which led me down into the cold, dark hole of emptiness and nothingness. I was constantly lost and felt worthless, while all I did was work and train while suppressing every thought that came into my head. It was easier for me just to keep pushing that shit down. If I told anyone, I'd just be complaining. Well, so I thought anyway.

I heard a quote that changed my perspective on life. That quote was from Tom Bilyeu: 'The only thing that matters in this life is what do you think about yourself when you're by yourself.'[15]

What do you think about yourself when you're by yourself? This blew my mind when I first heard it. Even the possibility that someone could sit by themselves and think about themselves without going crazy was far beyond anything imaginable for me at that time.

A couple of weeks passed, and I thought about the idea of sitting alone with my thoughts. But I was still too emotionally incapable and fearful of what might happen at this time. Until I could hear my heart trying to speak or send me messages, and I actually allowed myself to listen this time. I can't tell you how it snuck through the shield I had up, but it did and came at a great time.

It was a hot summer evening. I laid across a small single bed tucked into the corner of a 4x2 room at one of the rural job site camps where I lived and worked. I lay there, wide awake, tossing and turning, having another night where I couldn't fall asleep. Normally I would get up and walk around the camp or on the treadmill until I was exhausted, but this night I didn't. It wasn't long until I had this strong constant voice repeating this question:

## 'What Do I Want To Do With My Life?'

This is one of the most common issues I hear from my clients. 'I don't know what I want to do with my life' or 'how do I find my purpose in life?' It's not an easy question to answer, and it's definitely not something that I can give you the answer to; it must be discovered. Yes, discovered but not in the form of searching. You cannot 'find' your purpose; it will come to you when you become awakened. It will be right under your nose when you are ready for it. Signs and symbols will be your friend as your guide.

When people ask these questions, what they are really asking is, 'What can I do with my time that is important?' If our purpose gives our life meaning and happiness, and if we go back to what I covered at the start of this chapter – those important things we do are the ones that bring meaning and happiness to our lives. Then what our purpose should be is what leaves us happy and fulfilled.

If having a job you like and a family you love spending time with leaves you happy and fulfilled, then that's your purpose, no more and no less. If working hard for six months and then travelling for six months leaves you happy and fulfilled, then that's your purpose. If writing, playing an instrument, or playing a sport, leaves you happy and fulfilled, then that's your purpose.

This doesn't work for some men though, and the reason that so many men are living unhappy and unfulfilled lives is that they are searching in all the wrong places and for the wrong things. They attempt to find this fulfilment in things that give them the most personal gain and bring them the most comfort. Spending time searching for different external things they can take and bring into their lives instead of searching for the things they can give and provide value to others.

Giving is fundamental and inbuilt to human nature, and along with generosity, it has been a survival instinct that humankind has developed through evolution. In the act of giving back, it's scientifically proven that it will actually help you live a more fulfilled life.[16] So not only are you making other people's lives better, you're improving your own life by helping others. I know first-hand the truth in this and the dramatic increase in my sense of fulfilment that comes from transforming the lives of others.

It also fits in exactly with the Law of Attraction, what you put out, you get back in return. If you give, you are open to receiving. Holding onto things and not letting them go prevents anything from returning to you. This is also true regarding emotions, beliefs, negative patterns, behaviours and habits; if you hold onto them and don't let them go, you'll be blocking anything new or better coming into your life. This is more commonly referred to as self-sabotage.

### What Can You Give To The World?

Finding your purpose can be as simple as finding a way to help others and what you can ultimately give the world. As many self-centred men before us have come to realise and prove, is that confusing a self-centred existence with a purpose leads to unfulfillment and dis-satisfaction in life.

Let's take the story of John D. Rockefeller, for example. He thought he had lived his life in line with his purpose, but in reality, he was wrong. It sucked the life out of him, his health deteriorated, and it nearly cost him his life. He was lying on his death bed, almost everyone giving up on him. He received a revelation from God, which led him to a pivotal transition away from a 'taker' mindset to the mindset of a 'giver.'

After this moment, what happened next was remarkable. He slowly recovered, his body regained strength, his appetite improved, and he lived another 40 years. He provided value in others' lives via his wealth and personal talents and found his real purpose, which saved his life.

## Each & Every One of Us Has a Life's Purpose

I genuinely believe that every one of us has our own purpose, and I want you to discover yours. I know what it's like to be lost and alone. I know what it's like to have constant thoughts of not being good enough, which can make the process of finding something to give so damn hard if you feel like you have nothing to offer. The war within your own mind is the only one that you will ever need to win, and It's only ever you vs you. The war that's taking place right now is that one taking place in the absence of fulfilment and lack of purpose. Sometimes you need to look to others for help to become aware of what you are able to give.

I want you to know you have a future ahead of you. I want you to know you're smart, even if you may not meet the highest academic standards. I want you to know that you're just as good and valuable as any other human who happens to be born into a more privileged circumstance, even though there are so many mixed messages out there telling you otherwise. So, let this be your message, let this book be your pivotal transition, just like the one Rockefeller experienced.

The current mentality around men — and I was no exception to this — is that our life's purpose is out there, just waiting to be found. This is the same mentality as needing to 'find ourselves.' We search far and wide, looking, searching, hoping that one day we might just come across a realisation that reveals who we are and what our purpose is. That is where so many of us go wrong and why we end up in the relentless searching cycle that cannot be broken. In essence, we are sending ourselves on a wild goose chase of an unachievable mission.

## End the Wild Goose Chase.

I want you to consider that what you are searching for doesn't and will not come from anything outside of yourself. It must come from within you. See, you already know the things you are good at, as well as the things that give you the most fulfilment. But they are buried very deep down inside of you. Sometimes you are conscious of them, and sometimes you are not. Sometimes it might simply be too painful to confront them.

These things are within you, even though they may be buried ten layers deep. You have the ability to rediscover and retrieve all that is down there. There is no point in going out into the world seeking your purpose; it's already inside of you.

When you are lost and searching, it can lead you to go to desperate lengths to help in your search. If a man believes his purpose is outside of himself, he will end up on all sorts of spiritual, religious, meditation or yoga retreats. Heck, he may even find himself in the bush, naked, with no one around, thinking to himself, 'How the fuck did I end up here?'.

Only once you begin living life with this purpose that you have discovered within yourself can you begin to create a life full of joy, fulfilment, and success. What comes with this is the development of your own spiritual purpose through a set of values, principles, and beliefs that allow you to accept and build your unique meaning of life.

By now, you might be saying, 'Ok, so I know my purpose is something I enjoy, it's something I'm good at, it's something that leaves me fulfilled, and that something is already inside of me. But how do I uncover this thing?' Unfortunately, if you're in a place that is all too common among men, a place where you struggle to see what you are good at, what you enjoy, and what leaves you fulfilled. Well, what do you do in this situation? What do you do when your thoughts shut down every bit of self-worth or happiness?

## Passion

Your passions can be closely linked to your purpose. It goes without saying that your purpose is something that you are passionate about. So let's start with getting clear on your passion. Answer the following questions six questions.[17]

**Question #1:** Start by writing down what you don't like doing.

**Question #2:** List the jobs or tasks you dislike or even hate. Once you have eliminated these options, your real passion may become more evident

**Question #3:** Create a list of the people you are jealous of by asking the question, 'who do I envy the most because of the work they do.'

**Question #4:** List multiple individuals, then look at what they do and circle the jobs you would like.

**Question #5:** Eliminate anything on your 'jealous' list that is on your 'don't like' list that you don't like doing.

**Question #6:** The remaining circled information should provide clues about what can trigger your passion.

### Ask, and You Shall Receive

When it's hard to see for yourself through your worldview, you need to reach out. It is going to be humbling, and it's going to be hard. We, as men, are taught that asking for help is a sign of weakness. Let me tell you that you're reading this, which means you are out there searching, wanting, and asking for help. It doesn't need to stop here; ask, and you shall receive.

Here I'm going to give you a framework on which you can base your message and use it right now to reach out and finally get some answers to these questions. What you receive back might take time for you to grasp. You may have been telling yourself otherwise for a long time now, so at first, you might reject and throw that shield up, but I invite you to sit with these realisations, take them in and look through an expanded awareness of how that might be true.

**Framework:** *'Hi, this message might come as a surprise to you as I haven't been the type of man to ask for help all that often. Today I'm going to change that, and I'd really appreciate it if you could answer a couple of questions about me that would really help me out. The first one is, what do you think I'm good at? The second is, what do you think I'm not so good at? Lastly, what do you think is something that makes me truly happy? Again, thank you for your time answering these for me, and please be as honest as possible.'*

What you'll get out of this is feedback, a list of strengths and weaknesses from the important people in your life. I do not doubt that you will completely disagree with some of their thoughts. Everyone's version of reality is different, and your versions might not be aligned. This doesn't mean that your version is wrong, and it also doesn't mean that their version is wrong. Spend some time with your thoughts and let your mind make some discoveries. Make sure to follow the Third Pillar: assume nothing – we'll get to that later.

This is where the ultimate self-sabotage will occur when you start to assume that the things you do affect others' thoughts. Unless you have asked them and you can be 100% sure, do not assume.

Once you have gathered this feedback, or if you skipped that step, it's time to move on with further self-inquiry by asking yourself a few short questions. Harness the power in writing things down by now answering these questions below. Knowing what makes you happy and fulfilled will allow you to take strides into finding and living your purpose.

**Question 1.** What do I love to do?

**Question 2.** What am I good at?

**Question 3.** What are the two traits I most enjoy giving out to the world? For example: joy, loyalty, kindness, integrity.

**Question 4.** What are two ways I most enjoy expressing these traits?

---

## KEY POINTS

**POINT #1:** There are two specific hurdles that many of us get caught up on;

1. The 'need' for having a purpose

2. Thinking a purpose should be some big, world-changing resolution like solving 'world peace,' 'ending poverty,' or some extreme radical movement.

**POINT #2:** The biggest killer of your happiness is allowing others to be in control of your happiness.

**POINT #3:** Having others around you can add to your happiness, but they are not responsibly for it. Happiness comes from within; when your inner world is strong, nothing outside can affect you.

**POINT #4:** If a man continues searching for that higher purpose, a few things will happen;

1. He will fall into the constant cycle of searching but not finding.

2. He will think he's found his purpose until a realisation comes when it's not something that truly brings enjoyment and a sense of fulfilment to his life anymore, aka midlife crisis

3. He gives up on that search with the belief that 'I don't need a purpose' or 'I wasn't born to have a purpose like others are.

**POINT #5:** You cannot 'find' your purpose; it will come to you when you become awakened.

**POINT #6:** It will be right under your nose when you are ready for it.

**POINT #7:** The real question is, 'What can I do with my time that is important?'

**POINT #8:** Finding your purpose can be as simple as finding a way to help others and what you can ultimately give the world.

**POINT #9:** Knowing what makes you happy and fulfilled will allow you to take strides into finding and living your purpose.

# 8

## THE SUPERIOR

*"There is nothing noble in being superior to your fellow men. True nobility lies in being superior to your former self."*
**- Ernest Hemingway**

Over the last few decades, the world has begun shifting to a 50/50 economic and social equality between the masculine and the feminine. What is becoming more prevalent with this shift is the demasculinisation of males. Boys are becoming more girly, submissive, and 'pussified'. Boys are staying boys and are not growing up to be a man and this will continue to happen if men like you and me do not rise to this challenge. What happens if one of these fully grown 'boys' has their own son? He will be raised to be a boy. A man cannot be raised by a boy, and a man cannot be taught how to be a man by a boy! And so, this de-masculinisation continues indefinitely. If men don't become men, their sons will not become men either.

We can look at sperm counts, which halved between the 1930s and 1990s and have dropped an additional 1/3 since 1990. And what about testosterone levels? It has declined about 1% per year from 1980, while hormone replacement therapy has more than doubled from 2010 to 2013.[18] (Thomas G. Travison, 2007) So, there is no visible end to this de-masculinisation if we don't do something about it.

Masculinity is becoming a trait that is being beaten out of boys at a young age and is met with disapproval as they develop into young men. Any show of masculinity has somewhere been confused with the fucked-up 'modern-feminism' belief that all masculinity is 'toxic.' Young boys are severely punished for fighting, wrestling, or any type of aggression. Young boys are being taught at schools with mostly female teachers and raised in homes with almost non-existent fathers.[19] Societal beliefs and the media portray the need for men to become more in tune with their emotions and feminine sides. Yes, understanding your emotions, having emotional intelligence, and knowing it's ok to 'feel' instead of suppressing them is the key here. But what's happening is men are turning into these 'pussified' men who do not and can not take responsibility for their lives. I see it all the time. The number of no-shows I get from men telling me their life is so bad, and it's 10/10 important for them to want to fix it. Until I call (at a time they booked into my calendar, mind you), and there's no answer. Even after I send them a message beforehand, all they need to do is say 'no, I'm not interested'. This is just one example. But hey, it's not their fault; they probably didn't have the best role model of a father.

## Porn, Reality & Relationships

Porn and the ability to make proposals for sex on platforms like Tinder have taken away the drive for a man to put any effort into a lasting relationship, which would require work. There is no need for him to either grow up or 'man up' when instant gratification is only a few clicks away. Another possible outcome, if men don't have a father around, is the mother is forced to be the disciplinarian and the one in control, plus the one that gives us love. This is why boys can grow up with the unconscious perception that the ones who give them love – their partners – are also the ones that are in control.

See, our mothers are the first woman we fall in love with as we are born. Whether we like it or not, we look up to her for what we'd like in a future partner. Either compliant (similar) or defiant (opposite) traits in our mum are what you'll see in your partner. So if your mum is the 'enforcer,' and you're compliant, it's possible for you to unconsciously attract a partner that becomes just like your mum. A partner who you have to always 'run' things by without making decisions yourself. A partner who looks after you just like mum would. A partner who loses the sexual attraction towards you.

All this can lead to the development of insecure, non-competitive, weak men who can't seem to manage basic life skills and are incapable of actual human interaction. Walk down the street and look another man in the eyes; eight times out of ten, he will look away or look at the ground. We are raising weak men who cannot even look another man in the eyes.

### Eye to Eye

By no means was I any different. I would get so nervous looking anyone in the eye for more than 5 seconds, and I would get so uncomfortable in some situations that my nerves would cause me to be physically sick. Talk about incapable.

When I was twenty, a few school friends and I went out for a night on the town. From memory, it was a Wednesday night – cheap uni drinks, of course. This was back when I needed to drink to start any kind of conversation with anyone, let alone a female. Most of the memory is a bit vague, although the moment I recall the most was when I walked out of the men's toilet and around the corner, soon to be stopped by a group of people. It was like a human traffic jam until it happened; I got trapped. Standing there in front of me were two of the most beautiful woman I'd ever seen. My stomach dropped. I felt this chill come over my body. One of the girls started talking to me; I looked at her; I looked at the other, and I still have no idea what she said to me.

At that very moment, It felt like I was in a bubble; I couldn't hear, I couldn't speak, I couldn't do anything. The next thing I remember is running into the bathroom with my hand over my mouth, trying to stop the vomit from coming out. As you could imagine, I copped a bit of flack for others in the bathroom. I locked myself in the cubicle for what felt like an hour. I put my head down and walked straight to the taxi rank. It was a very low point for me, and it wasn't until I started doing the inner work in 2019 that I actually fully let go of that. I want to say if you're going through something similar, you can break free of this. If you'd like my help, just reach out to me.

### Separation, Divorce & Depression

Divorce is occurring more frequently than ever and becoming especially prevalent among men in their 40s and 50s, leading more men down the path of depression and suicide. These women have become so sick and tired of the pussies their husbands have become that it's easier for them to take the kids and pack up and leave, thinking, 'It will be so much easier on my own.' They would rather raise children alone than live with their doormat husbands. If they do hang around until the children have grown up, as soon as they can, they file for a divorce to now begin to 'live my life.' They leave men feeling like they have nothing, they have lost everything, and it gets too painful to think about continuing. This is partly because a man's whole life purpose has become his female partner. His partner has become his purpose.

Looking back, why did all my past relationships plummet towards separation? I was that weak, incapable, doormat, pussy of a man. I would complain and whine about everything, continuously picking on their flaws while completely neglecting my own huge faults. For most of one of my relationships, all I wanted to do was have sex. I didn't want to go anywhere, do anything apart from stay in the bedroom, and treat her like some sort of sex slave. Only to brag to my workmates how many times we did it over the weekend. What kind of asshole would do that? Looking back at that now, I don't know why that poor girl stuck around for so long.

For me to become the man that I am today, I had to die and be reborn. That man I speak about above is dead, and he died and has been reborn into a man that would beat out the old me every day in every aspect of body, mind, spirit, relationships, and profits. This is a mediocre man's rebirth and a Superior Man's awakening.

For decades, men have been known to be better providers and producers. If we look back to a century ago, this is definitely the case, but nowadays, women are becoming equal. Not the same, just equal. A man and a woman can never be the same, and they will never be the same, just like a penis and a vagina will never be the same. They can be equal, which is excellent. I'm all for equality. But they will never be the same.

## The Superior You

Let me be clear, when I talk about being the Superior Man, I'm not talking about being superior to anybody else: no other man or woman. Being superior is about living the fullest and the best version possible of yourself. Where you reach a place in which, essentially, you are the superior version of yourself. Although, understand that this place will never fully be reached. A Superior Man knows that he will continue to grow, and with that, his best version will continue to shift and advance.

Striving for perfection is never going to be the target. Continuous growth and striving for greatness are the ultimate outcome. Somewhere along the line, we have become caught up in the idea that something must be perfect. Perfection is not real, period. Thinking you or something around you must be perfect does nothing besides causing you tremendous amounts of unnecessary stress. What comes when the thoughts and the stories around the relationship with perfection are dropped? Can a whole new perspective be seen?

My obsession around perfection with my body caused me to live constantly with the stress of eating the 'perfect' diet, having the 'perfect' muscle recovery protocol, and having the 'perfect' training program. It became the self-destructive obsession of my life that I couldn't break free from. It fucked up nearly every other aspect of my life, from my relationships and social life to happiness and my mental and spiritual health. It was slowly changing how I looked at and operated inside my career.

## The Prison

In the book *The Unchained Man*, Caleb Jones makes the argument that men live inside a prison.[20] My study of some parts of the book led me to realise that men live behind bars constructed of their fears, outdated biology and societal beliefs. Many of which were constructed by powerful old men who are long dead. Any time a man tries to question any of these, the other inmates – fellow men inside this prison – will attempt to silence and shame that man for doing so. Inside this prison, your only role is to serve, operate, obey, and stay quiet.

The inmates of this prison conform to the societal beliefs that you must go to school, get a job, buy things you don't really need with money you don't have, all to impress people you don't even like. You choose and date one woman, you eventually get married to her, and you spend the following years following her orders because 'a happy wife equals a happy life.' You have 1.9 children before the age of thirty, and you buy a house. You may then get divorced, and your wife will take everything while you lose a lot of money and most likely yourself. You must be critical of and get angry at politicians, even if you elected them. Be angry and jealous of the rich, CEOs, bosses, and bankers. Save up and go on one vacation a year. Save for your retirement; if you haven't, expect your children and the government to look after you. If you decide not to do anything other than this, the other inmates hurl insults at you, telling you that you are selfish, egotistic, greedy, and immature. No one likes being called this, so you retreat back into the confined lines of the prison.

What comes with the transformation and awakening into the Superior Man is the escape from the confines of the prison. When you finally take a stand and say NO to the societal beliefs, NO to the old men and the beliefs they implanted, NO to the beliefs of the prison, and NO to the reality inside the prison. 'I'm no longer going to live my life to meet anyone else's expectations but my own.'

## The Ultimate War

I began to study the *Bhagavad Gita*[19], which is a part of the book of the scriptural trinity of Sanaatana Dharma, more commonly known as Hinduism. Inside this scripture is a story of the Supreme Lord, Krishna, his devotee-friend, Arjuna, and the war of Mahaabhaarata. There was an ancient king who had two sons, Dhritaraashtra and Paanda. The first son, Dhritaraashtra, who himself had 100 children that were known as the Kauravs. The second son, Paandu, had only five sons of his own, known as the Paandavs.

The kingdom was divided into two halves between the Kauravs and the Paandavs. But this wasn't enough for Duryodhana (the eldest of the Kauravs), who wanted the whole kingdom to himself, much like many old men who had started wars if you were to look back over history.

Arjuna and the other Paandavs did not want war, but it ultimately proved to become unavoidable, and this left the Paandavs with just two options: to fight or to run.

One of the five Paandavs brothers, Arjuna, later faced the ultimate dilemma within himself on the battlefield: whether he, too, should fight or run away to preserve the peace and nonviolence. Arjuna, being the great warrior he was – one of the greatest India ever had – thought he only had one choice. He knew he needed to claim the kingdom back, which would require him to go to battle.

Down at the battlefield of Kurukshetra near New Delhi, Lord Krishna had descended in disguise to whiteness one of the greatest battles in India's history, and he wanted to be right in the thick of it.

Arjuna got down off his chariot, ready for battle, and looked across the battlefield to see his most admired gurus, his cousins, uncles, grandfathers, teachers, and brothers all fighting for the opposing Army. At this moment, Arjuna broke down, knowing that his Army was more powerful than theirs, and he would kill them all. He wanted to surrender. He did not want to fulfil his duties as a warrior, which were all too hard for him to deal with.

The rest of the seven hundred verse scripture becomes a dialogue between Lord Krishna guiding the confused Arjuna on the battlefield. Krishna goes on to teach Arjuna that the real battle he is facing isn't the external battle but rather the internal battle within himself. He guides Arjuna through the darkness of his mind, leading Arjuna into the light inside himself. This internal struggle was the ultimate war he had to face.

Arjuna's dilemma is, for most, the same as every other human being. The war is not outside. The battle is within. After studying the Gita, I realised that what I was searching so hard to find was not anything outside of me. It never was and never will be. What I was searching for had to come from within. My internal struggles were the solutions that were going to set me free.

## Escaping the Prison

Learning from Arjuna and the Gita, the only way to escape the prison is by addressing the internal conflicts you have inside your own mind about leaving the prison behind. Any societal beliefs you hold must be questioned for their truth and your own internal beliefs surrounding them. The ultimate war is won and lost inside, and the Superior Man questions and wins the ultimate war.

The first time I was awoken to this idea of questioning your beliefs, I was sitting in a classroom on the other side of the country. A few weeks earlier, I had been told by a work colleague that I should look into this as it's what he thought I needed to do and that it would really help me. I was making a few thousand-dollar investment into an NLP & Time Line Therapy® practitioner course that I knew nothing about and had until then never even heard of. I just listened to the voice inside me that said, 'Go' and so I did.

Still trying to work out why I was even there and already had run through a thousand different stories and excuses of why not to go. I walked in that first morning and was introduced to Paul Eliseo. He was the first person to open my mind and explain where my beliefs came from. Meeting Paul has been a pivotal point in my life and has allowed me to change the course of my life.

## The Reality of Problems

We were sitting having this conversation when he said to me, 'show me your problems.' My first thought was, 'Where do I even start?'

'See this imaginary circle on the ground', Paul asked, and he used his hands to draw a circle on the floor. 'Show me your problems and put them in there. Go on; I'll wait'. I didn't know what to do or say. My problems were in my head, so how was I supposed to get them out and put them on the ground? Again, he said, 'Show me your problems and put them in there.'

Sitting there, not knowing what I was meant to be doing, Paul went on to explain that the problems and issues we face are nothing but our own reality. These problems aren't real problems. We think they are, and they might seem to us like they're really fucked-up issues, but the reality is that the issues and the problems we have don't come from that. They are a result of a belief we have about a past event. That belief fuels the stories inside us to cause stress, worries, and more problems or challenges. Your past, or your version of the past, only exists in one place, your mind.

We dive deeper into these conversations later on, but for now, understand that you must be willing to question your beliefs and your reality to transform into the Superior Man and escape the confines of the prison.

### Every Moment Waited is a Moment Wasted

The common misconception among men is the idea that one day, what they want will be done. They think, ' If I work hard when I'm younger, I'll be able to work less and rest when I'm older.' Or, 'I'm only doing this now while I'm young so I can do what I want later on.' Or, 'I'll be happy once I make x amount of money or once I find the female I'm looking for or once I become successful.' It's a mistake to think that eventually, all things will be different or that you'll be happy as soon as you reach a specific place.

It's never going to end; it's never going to be over. If you're not happy now, you won't be happy after getting that one thing you're looking for. Stop thinking it will be better or easier in the future. If anything, it will get harder. For now, spend an hour a day doing the thing that you are waiting to do, just until you are more financially secure or your children have moved out or until you feel free to do the thing you want to do. Don't wait any longer to do the things that you love to do. Do the things that you are waiting to do, and do the things that you have been born to do. Live up to the things that the Superior You has the potential to do.

If you can't find the time, make the time, and if you *still* can't find the time, question if it is actually something you want to do. If it's not, that's fine. Drop the thought and move on. When I first started building AMD, I was already working 55-60 hours a week in my job as a civil supervisor, and I was also spending a further 20-30 hrs a week on AMD. I would get asked why am I doing this, and don't you ever get bored? I would reply that I enjoyed everything I was doing with AMD. I can have the worst day at work and come home and do 6hrs work in half the time on AMD. It was my purpose and my passion, and it was the highest on my list of values. It still is to this day.

Yes, I definitely thought that things would be better once I reached a place where I could afford to quit my job and pursue this full-time, but I was staying true to spending an hour or more a day on the thing I wanted to do, and I loved every moment of the journey. With every struggle and every win, I was happy. It all comes down to the fact that short-term sacrifices are needed when you can see an end goal.

### Don't Wait, Take Action

I had a client who came to see me with overwhelming anxiety, which had come on a few years earlier. For years, he had his head down in a job that didn't fulfil him, but he knew it paid the bills. He believed he just needed to pay his house off, and then he'd be free. He'd be able to travel. He'd be able to find a job he enjoyed, and he'd be able to finally follow his purpose.

In 2020, he reached his goal of paying the house off, and it was nothing like he expected. In his words, 'we walked into the bank to pay the loan off, and not one person said congratulations. All they did was ask if we'd like to borrow more.' That was a big letdown to him as it was nowhere near the expectation he'd visualised in his head.

Not long after that, Covid hit. Everything got shut down; borders closed, which meant no more travel. His brother got stuck with him, so he was worried about him getting back to the UK to be with his family. It was also not a good time to be changing careers. So you can see, for 25 years, his motivation had been head down, paying this loan off while disregarding what he wanted. Thinking once it is paid off, he can then do the things he wanted to do and find his purpose. Once he did actually pay the loan off, it wasn't as big of a deal as he thought it would be. Plus, with Covid and all the things happening at that time, this fuelled his worry and anxiety whenever he thought about the future.

If he had done things for himself 25 years ago, he might not have been in this position. I also uncovered he was motivated by fear, e.g. fear of not being able to pay the house off, which did serve him for a long time. But now, as he looked forward into the future, he got anxious because he didn't know what he was doing. On top of that, because he was motivated by fear, he'd look for all the things that could go wrong in the future. So it became a cycle between anxiousness and fear. This was why it became so overwhelming for him.

The anxiety-fear cycle made it seem like he's always negative and constantly focused on the negatives. Fear = negatives. So it was just his strategy for action. If you are someone that focuses on the negatives, this story might open your awareness as to why.

### Abundance vs. Scarcity

The Superior Men who have lived abundant lives are men who have never waited for anything. They haven't waited for money, for security, for things to be easier, or for women to enter their lives. I believe every man has a gift to give the world, a gift to give their woman, and a gift to give themselves. Every moment waited is a moment wasted, and each wasted moment destroys your clarity of purpose, happiness, and fulfilment.

When a man lives in scarcity, he is a passenger inside his own life; he is not driving the bus. Scarcity comes when we can't get or don't have enough of something desirable, such as money, sex, energy, jobs, etc. Therefore, that item gets put on a pedestal. This is why many men get so nervous about meeting, attracting, and engaging with females, and I was definitely one of them. It all starts around the time of our early teens when the belief around sex is that it is often scarce and hard to come by. This then fuels the belief that we must be careful of what we do and say around females. A few years later, this scarcity mindset subconsciously affects how we act and sabotages our chances with the women we meet.

The Superior You lives in abundance. This might be a hard concept to take hold of, as it goes against some of your beliefs, beliefs formed by the societal prison that will require internal reprogramming to break free from.

If you only had one year left to live, would you be living the life you are right now? 'Thank god it's Friday' is a term used way too often. Yes, it's the weekend, and you get a couple of days off, but the problem lies when Monday comes around, and you already wish for it to be Friday again. Essentially you are wishing away 70% of your life. If you take the average life span of a male, which is 78 years old, 30% of that is 23 and a half years, remove a further third for the time we sleep, and you end up with 15.5 years. Out of 78 years, you only want to live and enjoy the 15.5 years of your weekends. This is where you need to assess your life and say, 'Fuck that!' I'm going to live the fullest life I can. Take the actions you need to take to start enjoying every day you're alive. If you need a complete overhaul of your life, then do that. As stuck in your current life as you may think you are, there's always a way out.

To reach the Superior You, you must be willing to shed the man you are today and let go of his beliefs, values, problems, ultimate wars, and internal battles. There will be resistance from others around you, and I can ensure you that most of it will come from inside your mind; it won't be easy, but it is definitely possible and worth it. I know for a fact that this system, the MMC, works, and it all comes down to one thing. You, my friend. You are the only one that can do it. Apply everything inside this code, and the Superior You will be awakened and activated.

## KEY POINTS

**POINT #1:** Over the last few decades, there's been a shift towards a de-masculinisation of males. Boys are becoming more girly, submissive, and 'pussified'.

**POINT #2:** A man cannot be raised by a 'fully grown boy', and a man cannot be taught how to be a man by a boy!

**POINT #3:** Masculinity is becoming a trait that is being beaten out of boys at a young age and is met with disapproval as they develop into young men. Any show of masculinity has somewhere been confused with the fucked-up 'modern-feminism' belief that all masculinity is 'toxic.'

**POINT #4:** Porn and the ability to make proposals for sex on platforms like Tinder have taken away the drive for a man to put any effort into a lasting relationship, which would require work.

**POINT #5:** If your mum is the 'enforcer,' and you're compliant, it's possible for you to unconsciously attract a partner that becomes just like your mum. A partner who you have to always 'run' things by without making decisions yourself. A partner who looks after you just like mum would. A partner who loses the sexual attraction towards you.

**POINT #6:** Being superior is about living the fullest and being the best version possible of yourself.

**POINT #7:** The real battle we face isn't the external battle but rather the internal battle within ourselves.

**POINT #8:** When a man lives in scarcity, he is a passenger inside his own life; he is not driving the bus.

**POINT #9:** This scarcity mindset subconsciously affects how we act and sabotages our chances with the women we meet.

**POINT #10:** You must be willing to shed the man you are today and let go of his beliefs, values, problems, ultimate wars, and internal battles.

# 9

## THE FORGIVENESS

*"The greatest deception men suffer is from their own opinions."*
**- Leonardo da Vinci**

For a man to learn to forgive and let go, it can take years, sometimes even as long as a lifetime. Forgiveness is a challenge for everyone; it can even seem impossible in some situations. Forgiveness isn't about the other person involved; forgiveness is something that you do by yourself and for yourself.

Whenever someone has wronged you, or you've been pissed off, a massive shift occurs inside you. What happens is that your power and energy are taken from you and directed toward this person or situation. So, what we are doing here is allowing you to forgive yourself so that you can reclaim your power and energy back from this person or situation. You will never be able to forgive others if you cannot forgive yourself first.

'Let go in order to grow.' That statement was something I kept hearing, replayed over and over again inside my head. The more I heard it, the more confused I felt. 'What the fuck is letting go, and what do I even need to let go of?' The voice continued to give me this message even though I couldn't find the answer anywhere.

That is until one morning, I woke up with my head pounding as though I'd been hit by a train, and I immediately remembered what had happened the night before. I was embarrassed, ashamed, and shocked that something like this could have happened. All I wanted to do was close my eyes and never wake up again. For days afterwards, I was constantly beating myself up about it. From the outside, it would have looked like I belonged in a mental institute or somewhere similar. It was around the fifth day of this continuous internal destruction that I had the liberating realisation.

## Just Let Go

This time the voice spoke, and I just listened. Just… Let… Go… It came with the realisation that I needed to forgive myself before anyone else could forgive me. The lack of forgiveness toward myself would have blocked any forgiveness from anybody else.

Now let me get this clear, this is not some new-age hype or feel-good motivational talk about forgiveness. You can pick up any book, search for any article, or watch any YouTube video on forgiveness to learn how to forgive. This is not about that. This is about being able to forgive and let go of who you are and how you have got to the place you are in right now.

As we look through our past, many of us think back to the times we really messed up, the times that we wish never happened, and the things we wish we could take back. We then live with regret inside a reality where self-forgiveness does not exist. A lack of self-worth, a lack of self-respect, and a lack of self-esteem all stem from the lack of our ability to just let go and forgive ourselves.

The continuous internal abuse and negative thoughts about ourselves lead us to determine that we are bad men, which can drive us down the dark and lonely road of depression and suicidal thoughts. Being our worst enemy and our harshest critic makes this process so damn hard to break free of. If you can allow yourself to be forgiven, you will be more motivated to change as a man. The ability to forgive yourself loosens the shackles you have chained around you and opens you up to new possibilities and levels.

Whatever you have done in your past and whatever you have done to get to where you are right now are all a part of you and have made you who you are. We are not trying to forget that. Forgiving isn't forgetting. There's a misconception around forgiveness that we must 'forgive and forget'. Forgetting only means suppressing and nothing else. You can never and will never be able to forget anything. Why, might you ask?

## The Gorilla

Forgetting might be something you think you can do in your conscious mind, but it will never happen in your unconscious mind. That gorilla in the room is your unconscious mind, and it remembers everything. 95% of your brain is made up of your unconscious mind.[21] It isn't creative, it doesn't make jokes, and it doesn't know sarcasm. It simply remembers everything you have ever done, said, heard, seen, and witnessed.

Every event, situation, and memory is stored in the mind as images. These images of events get stored like a big filing cabinet inside your mind right back to when you were in your mother's belly.

So, if you can't truly forget and don't forgive, these thoughts and events get suppressed to the point where they are like a loaded gun, ready to unleash on anybody around us. Unfortunately, the people we are closest to and love the most, find themselves in the firing line more often than not. This suppressed anger, frustration, rage, sadness or whatever else we feel comes out like an explosion in road rage, king-hits, punched walls, thrown phones, violent outbursts, verbal abuse; I could go on forever.

## Forgiving is Not Forgetting

Be grateful for what you have done in your past to be here where you are right now. If you didn't do that one thing you regret, you might not be sitting here reading this. Whether that be good or bad is neither here nor there. You are here to let go of that regret, let go of anything you are beating yourself up about, and finally, have that faith you need to forgive yourself and free your mind from this internal trap.

Making mistakes is how we learn best. But when we make a mistake as an adult in life, for some reason, we regret it. I want to propose a question to you. Would you regret it if you got a maths question wrong in grade 5? Or would you keep trying and making more mistakes until you finally learn how to do it?

The same is with life. We need to make mistakes to learn and grow. If we aren't making mistakes, we aren't pushing ourselves enough. Also, just like the maths question, you'll keep getting the same challenges or problems in life until you learn from them and move on. Once you learn from it, you won't need to repeat it.

What happens when we look back at an event and regret what we've done? We are looking back and beating ourselves up. Instead, we look back to grow, learn and move forward. Life is one big lesson, and if you keep getting the same lessons and challenges in life, you are not growing.

If you keep getting cheated on, you must learn something from that, so it stops. If you keep getting sacked, you must learn something from that so you can keep a job. If you keep getting put down or spoken over, you must learn something from that so that it stops.

Forgive yourself for everything you have done up until this point. Forgive yourself for every wrongdoing. For every person you have hurt, in every situation you didn't do what you could have done, for everything in your life. Let go of that resentment you hold against yourself and let go of that man you are right now.

## Now You Can Let Go in Order to Grow

Every one of those little situations, events, thoughts, and self-beliefs is like an anchor trying to hold you down, keeping you from reaching those next targets and expanding your kingdom. This is where the true meaning of letting go lies. Your ability to cut that cord to the anchor and be free from that burden and grow!

What allows this to be possible is you forgiving yourself. Forgiveness, more importantly, self-forgiveness, is what allows you to cut this cord and leave it behind. Not to forget about it; no, it's still there to be a reminder of who you were and who you needed to become in order to cut that cord. The man you needed to become.

There comes the point in our lives, and for you — it might be at this very moment — where we need to and must let go. We need to let go of the past: the hurt, the failures, the losses, the negative beliefs, the pain, suffering, hopes, and dreams. It is impossible to continue moving forward in life if we constantly hold on to something from our past. Letting go doesn't mean giving up. Letting go is not quitting. Letting go does not mean that you do not have the knowledge of what or how to do it. Letting go does not mean that you are incapable and powerless. Being able to let go simply means that you are aware that to reach a new height and experience anything new, better, or different, you must first let go.

I want you to consider that everything you have been beating yourself up about, including all those things that you haven't yet forgiven yourself for, is, in fact, a lie. I'll also have you consider that you might be able to see they are false by asking one simple question...

## 'Is It True?'

Can you be absolutely 100% sure that the situation you are describing to yourself is true? This is the path to freeing yourself from your unforgiving mind. You might have hurt someone physically. You might have broken the law. You might have done something bad. Ok, great; you'll be able to let go of that event. The thing that is holding you back from forgiving yourself is what you think the impact this has on others —is shame, guilt, embarrassment, humiliation, disgrace, and dishonour. We begin to make assumptions about what others are thinking, which further drives this. We discuss making assumptions further in Part II – The 5 Pillars.

We think others will be ashamed of us, we think others will hate us, and we think others will be disgusted with us, but this is where you must ask: is it true? Can you really know that what they are thinking is true? If you answer yes, ask again, and dig deeper; the answer will be no. When you come to this realisation, I'll have you consider what might be possible for you without the thought of what you think they are thinking of you? Who might you be able to be? Who might you be able to become? This is where self-forgiveness lies.

## Turn the Key to Forgive

Let's go one step deeper. The story you are telling yourself about what you assume someone is thinking is the exact feeling you have towards yourself. That person isn't ashamed of you; you are ashamed of yourself. That person isn't angry at you; you are angry at yourself. That person doesn't hate on you; you hate on yourself. That person isn't disgusted with you; you are disgusted with yourself. What you have found here is the very thing that is preventing you from forgiving yourself, and it is also the key which you must turn to access forgiveness.

What you have done in life up to this point is all that you could have done. How? Because it's what you have known best. You don't know what you don't know. You may look back now and think you could have done better, and that's a good sign, and it shows you've grown.

Where you are standing right now is a sum of what you have done, and this place is simply where you are. No more, no less. It's not bad, and it's not good; it just is. When we look back, we tend to have things we have labelled as 'bad' and things that we couldn't do right.

Let go of this idea of being right or wrong and decide to go after freedom and liberation rather than just trying to be right. We all mess up, we all make mistakes, and we always get things wrong, so let go of that belief that we must be right all of the time.

## Accept, Forgive & Liberate Yourself

This now brings us to the point where you must let go of the man you currently are, let go of this unforgiving man, let go of the good and bad and let go of who you were. Forgive yourself for everything you have done up until now but still be grateful for who you are.

Today, tonight, this morning, this evening, tomorrow, and as you continue along this journey, as you begin to be reborn as the modern man you desire, it all starts with you. With your willingness to forgive, with your willingness to let go, and with your willingness to find liberation and personal freedom.

My brother, welcome to this place of freedom, welcome to this place of acceptance and welcome to this movement.

## KEY POINTS

**POINT #1:** Forgiveness isn't about the other person involved; forgiveness is something that you do by yourself and for yourself.

**POINT #2:** You will never be able to forgive others if you cannot forgive yourself first.

**POINT #3:** A lack of self-worth, a lack of self-respect, and a lack of self-esteem all stem from the lack of our ability to just let go and forgive ourselves.

**POINT #4:** Forgiving isn't forgetting.

**POINT #5:** Consider that everything you have been beating yourself up about, including all those things that you haven't yet forgiven yourself for, is, in fact, a lie.

**POINT #6:** 'Is it true?' Can you be absolutely 100% sure that the situation you are describing to yourself is true?

**POINT #7:** As you continue along this journey, as you begin to be reborn as the modern man you desire, it all starts with you. With your willingness to forgive, with your willingness to let go, and with your willingness to find liberation and personal freedom.

# 10

# THE FACTS, FEELINGS & FIBS

*"All truth passes through three stages.
First, it is ridiculed. Second, it is
violently opposed. Third, it is accepted
as being self-evident."*
**- Arthur Schopenhauer**

There's a trifecta that is going on inside our minds that is made up of three parts, the facts, the feelings, and the fibs. They are constantly getting mixed together and distorting how a man sees the world, how he acts, and his ability to expand his life. To determine how all these apply to you, we must first consider and take a deeper look into these three main parts.

## Facing the Facts

Facts are facts; they are what is. They are data points. They are also not necessarily good or bad. They are simply what is going on in your life at this moment. What I have done = facts, what I haven't done = facts, what I think about = facts, what I want = facts, how I feel = facts.

It's difficult to just sit back while being in a completely neutral place and look at the facts and the truths as they are and as you see them. The challenge amongst us — you might be at this point now — is that these facts are becoming harder and harder to see. We suppress and cover these facts with the thought that facing reality is too hard to bear. The only way you will become the man you want to be is to learn to love and look for the facts. It is not because it makes you some personal development whizz or connected with some higher spiritual power, but because it is essential to your ability to expand and create as a man.

It's so much easier for most men to ignore the facts and pretend that nothing is going on than it is to face up to the problem. They run and ignore all the facts in their lives. If you cannot deal with the current facts and your life's current reality, then there is no hope in Hell that you will ever be able to create a new reality for yourself.

I see it happening everywhere every day. Men do something wrong; they cause something to happen or do something that affects someone else. Instead of taking ownership and accepting that they have stuffed up, they pretend they didn't do anything or don't know what happened. At the same time, they are pulling a cover over their eyes and telling themselves a made-up bullshit story about what is really going on.

It happens on social media, with couples discussing how happy they are together, only to reach out a few weeks later, thanking everyone for the support during their break-up. They carefully hand-select one out of every 1000 photos taken to show only the best bits of their lives while portraying 'This is the real me.' No it is not! You are covering up what your life really is like. Posting a photo showing you cooking a 'clean' meal or doing their weekly meal prep, only to eat a big dirty hamburger the next day, claiming that it's a 'cheat day'. Don't get me wrong; I have nothing against anyone posting anything on social media. What you do is completely up to you. But when you ignore the actual facts and reality of your life by publicly displaying a fake narrative, all you are doing is trying to convince your own mind that these are the new facts.

You see it further when you hear of men being cheated on for 5-10 years. A man came to me looking for help, saying that his wife had been cheating on him for the last five years. I told him that day, 'So, you are telling me that your wife has been cheating on you for the past five years, and you had no idea? There was not one moment where you thought that something was odd? All those late-night drinks with friends.' I finally called him out on his bullshit story and told him that he had been pretending it wasn't happening.

How about when men receive news of health issues like heart problems, high blood pressure, and diabetes, only to act as though they hadn't seen it coming. Meanwhile, this man has a stomach the size of a small child and has been gaining weight rapidly over the last few years, and he claims that he hadn't noticed. Stop pretending that shit in your life isn't happening.

## The Truth Will Set You Free

That might have been a slap in the face for some of you, but that's why I'm here. To extract these truths out from within because ultimately, the truth will set you free. So, are you ready to get real with the facts inside your life? Are you ready to accept that what it will take to be honest with yourself will change how your current reality impacts you? Pull out your Revelation Report, aka journal, and write exactly what is happening inside your life.

### Disconnecting the Feelings

What makes separating the facts from the situations so damn hard is the feelings that get attached to all those facts. The reason we hide from the facts is not due to the facts themselves. It's those feelings and emotions attached that we don't know how to deal with. How do we tell someone that our life isn't working? How do we tell someone what our deepest desires are? How do we tell someone about the problems that we are facing? How do we deal with the facts?

I can tell you of a time when I knew that my world was imploding when my mental state was rapidly declining, yet I tried to hide this from myself in the hope that it would go away. Whenever I thought of what might happen, it would push me further down the suppressive downward spiral of denial.

I can also tell you a time when I knew something was going on with a girlfriend and another guy, but I turned a blind eye, pretending to be ignorant of the situation, as I feared a break-up.

There was also a time when I wasn't happy and felt that my life wasn't 'working', so I decided to pack up and leave the country, hoping to run away forever and never have to come back to a world I thought I was stuck in and come back to the painful life I thought I was living.

I share all these facts openly with you. To show we all go through shit, we all have facts with feelings attached, which lead us to tell a bullshit story. Not to purposely hurt us, but to protect ourselves. These stories are directly linked to the feelings we have. To separate these, letting go of the feelings is what is needed to be learned. It's not an easy task; it takes a mentality shift of what being a man and suppressing our feelings was before you were introduced to the MMC.

Right now, you do not hold the capacity to release and separate these feelings, but once you do, your life becomes exciting, and you are not stuck living the same old way, constantly being and getting in your own way. It becomes possible for you to accept your feelings and acknowledge them without the attachment of a story.

It wasn't until I told myself, 'Stop Lying! Brendon, Stop Fucking Lying!' that I realised what it would take for me to tell the truth about the facts and the feelings. This was what I needed to get through the door that was standing in the way. For so long, I thought I needed to find a key, to find a clue as to how I could free myself from my thoughts, fibs, lies, and stories. It wasn't that I couldn't find them; it wasn't that I was looking in the wrong places, and it had nothing to do with anything outside of me. Being honest and truthful around the facts, the feelings, and the fibs and telling the truth was what gave me the focus to find my way through this door. This door was open the whole time. There was no key that I needed to find or search for. I just had to push it open.

No matter how lost or broken and beaten down you may feel, the truth will set you free no matter how unhappy your life is. The truth will push that door open for you. This goes deeper than the simple decision not to tell lies. It means speaking about the things that are going on in your life. Just accepting something the way it is and suppressing the emotions around this is not being honest. It's not allowing you to let the truth do its work.

### The Biggest Lie

'How are you?' 'I'm good.' 'How was your meal?' 'It was good.' 'How is your life?' 'It's good.' 'How is your health, how are your relationships, how is your career?' 'They're good.'

Your entire world might be burning to the ground, and the answer is still, 'I'm good.'

The time I realised this to its full extent was when I went out to dinner one night. The service was terrible, they had forgotten one meal and stuffed up another two, and there wasn't an apology from anywhere. That was the topic for most of the night, how bad that restaurant was. Once everyone had finished, a different waiter came over to clear the table. Once arriving, she asked, 'how was the meal?'. Nearly everyone at the table said it was good. It was good? Are you kidding me? That was the worst experience I think I'd ever had, but the response was still 'good'.

This is the sedated world we live in. Believing the story, I'll upset the waiter or look like I'm making a big deal if I say something. Not saying something, as I said before, is still lying. The stories we tell ourselves are fuelled by the feelings we are feeling and completely disregard the actual facts.

This trifecta of the facts, the feelings, and the fibs that disregard the truth is causing the greatest problems amongst men like you and me. The alignment of this trifecta brings a man to start climbing the mountain where his kingdom is built. These self-destructive fibs and stories draw so much of a man's energy that it becomes almost impossible to do anything great in his life. Letting go of these stores, fibs and thoughts begin the transfer of energy from self-destruction to giving him focus and clarity around who he is and who he wants to become.

This now sets the groundwork for introducing a tool that allows you to shift the story attached to feelings. You might start to realise that these stories you are telling about your feelings directly result from the stories you are telling or not telling about the facts. We'll discuss this further and how your stories ultimately mess you up. No, it's not you. It's your stories.

That tool is what is known here as 'The Flip'. These Flips allow you to take your current story and flip it towards a new desired story that does one thing: it finds freedom.

## KEY POINTS

**POINT #1:** There's a trifecta that is going on inside our minds that is made up of three parts, the facts, the feelings, and the fibs.

**POINT #2:** They are constantly getting mixed together and distorting how we see the world and how we act.

**POINT #3:** The only way you will become the man you want to be is to learn to love and look for the facts.

**POINT #4:** It's so much easier for most men to ignore the facts and pretend that nothing is going on than it is to face up to the problem.

**POINT #5:** If you cannot deal with the current facts and your life's current reality, then there is no hope in Hell that you will ever be able to create a new reality for yourself.

**POINT #6:** No matter how lost or broken and beaten down you may feel, the truth will set you free no matter how unhappy your life is. The truth will push that door open for you.

# 11

# THE FLIPS

*"Change will not come if we wait for some other person or some other time. We are the ones we've been waiting for. We are the change that we seek."*
**- Barack Obama**

For six years, I searched far and wide for the answers as to why I always seemed to mess things up. The conversations I had, the explanations I was giving, the disagreements or arguments I'd find myself in, and the female interactions I'd have always ended the same way: with me walking away, awkward, confused, lost, defeated, and sometimes embarrassed. I could not work out why I sucked so much, even after reading article, after article.

If you're here reading this, it probably means that you too are one of those men who frequently stuff things up. So, congratulations, and welcome to this place where we fuck up and make mistakes.

Now the reality is you're not the only one, and there's not a man on this earth who doesn't. Here's the thing, it doesn't matter how often we mess up; that's not the problem we have here. It's the stories and lies we get caught up in telling ourselves that are the problem, not the fuck-up itself.

These stories become the reason why we live a life of suffering. The suffering that is going on in our minds isn't actually reality. It's a story we torture ourselves with, as Byron Katie has described. You only suffer when you believe these stories to be true. When you don't, you won't suffer. But this is where the problem lies. We all tell stories every single day. Not a day goes by when we don't tell them, and once we've told them, we start to believe they are completely true.

### Arguing with Reality

If you want your reality to be different to its current state, you might as well try to fly to the sun. This simply isn't going to happen, and it is the exact same when you try to argue with the way reality is. To be clear, I'm not talking about changing your reality. I'm talking about arguing with it. You can change your reality once you see it the way it is, and arguing with it is where the suffering lies.

If you were to become more aware of the stories you tell daily, you would probably start to notice that you are arguing with your reality numerous times a day. 'I should be more confident.' 'My kids should do XYZ.' 'My wife or partner should listen to me more.' 'I should be making this much money or have this job.' 'I shouldn't get so angry.' These stories are all ways you want your reality to be different. You are arguing with reality. It can be depressing thinking about those stories, and you're right. It is depressing, and it's why so many men do end up depressed. Everything we feel and suffer here is because of the fact that we are arguing with reality.

I was introduced to a woman by the name of Byron Katie and her book *Loving What Is*[22], a remarkable discussion around the teachings she calls 'The Work.' Her teachings and insights around the stories we tell ourselves and our thoughts have caused an unfathomable quantum shift in my reality. Based on Byron's teachings formula, we'll discuss and break down what is known as 'The Flips' here inside AMD.

You and I have thousands of stories that pass through our minds every day. Most of them are just thoughts, passing as soon as the next one comes along. However, if a story gets a belief behind it, it can cause suffering. These stories could be about the past, present, or future. They could be about something that we should or shouldn't be, that they could or couldn't be, or simply why something is the way it is. It can be extremely stressful when we attach a belief to these stories, especially because when we believe them to be true, it takes a lot for us to lose our belief in them.

Years ago, when I was working on a mine site and living in the onsite camp, I shared a room with a guy who was about 20 years older than me. Every time he left the room, he would always leave the door open. I couldn't understand why he would walk out and not shut the door. I mean, how hard was it? Did he live in a tent? I repeated to myself on numerous occasions. One evening, after a few months of having to shut the door for him, I had finally had enough, and I decided to say something. I got up out of bed, ran outside, and shut the door behind me. I couldn't see which way he had gone, so I told myself, 'I'll say something when I get back.' I turned around and noticed that the door was open. At first, I couldn't understand why. I tried to close it again, but it wouldn't shut. I began to laugh as I realised that the lock was broken and that the door could only be closed from the inside.

For the past six months, I had been stressing, causing myself this internal rage over this man's inability to shut the door, only to realise that the door was the problem, not him. I was so caught up in the story around this man not shutting the door that my complete reality around it was focused on this one outcome, blinding me to the truth. More than likely, the same thing must have been happening to him. He either knew the door didn't shut, or he thought it was me who never shut the door. It's funny now.

### 'Is It True?'

This one simple question elevated my entire worldview. I started to question every part of reality and every story I had believed to be true. This simple question started to set me free as I began to see the light. The first big realisation occurred when the thought, 'I will never be good enough' came into my consciousness. I asked myself, 'Is it true?' Is it true that I will never be good enough? I was just about to say yes when I got a clear answer from the voice inside, 'No.' It was at that moment that I had a massive shift. It was here when I first experienced what it was like to shift my internal state.

I fell to the ground, a sense of relief pouring out of me. Kneeling there on my hands and knees, it was like I had dropped half my body weight. My shoulders became sore as if I'd just finished another one of my intense suppressive workouts. I was beside my bed, and I somehow fell asleep in this position. I'm guessing due to my sheer mental and emotional release.

I woke up the next day, and I was smiling. I replayed the words 'I am good enough' in my head for the next few hours, and I didn't want to leave that moment.

I'd like to now introduce you to The Flip, particularly The Self Flip. We have developed 16 Flips, including The Anger, Fear, Anxiety, Resentment, Guilt, Shame, Grief, Loss, Frustration, Insecure, Judgment,

Sadness, Self-Doubt, Obsession and Gaint Flips, which are not discussed here. To access the full Advanced Flips Personal Freedom Tools inside The AMD App, go to www.brendongiebel.com/amd-app.[23] We are also documenting and recording the things you can look back on to learn and teach for generations to come as you build and leave your legacy. Inside the AMD Brotherhood, we call this the King's Journal.

## The Power of The Written Word

As we dive further into The Flip, you'll notice that all we are doing is answering questions along the way. There's a power in the fact that when you put pen to paper or type it out, you are extracting the facts out of the story. If you try to answer these questions internally and in your mind, your mind will shut down any thoughts as quickly as possible when you go against the initial belief. Your mind will fight you every step of the way, not because it's against you, but just because that's what you've led it to believe. The way around this? Write it down. Your mind can't spin around words you've written like it can with your thoughts.

## The Self Flip

I've noticed that this is one of the most commonly used Flips when introduced to the new concepts and tools around The Flips. As we go through this, you will already have a story in your mind that pops out at you as soon as you start going through this. Great, grab a pen and go through your own Flip as we go along.

**Question #1:** What is the self-judgment you are telling yourself?

*Answer:* I am/should/can't etc _____ (self-judging thought) _____.

Think back to one of those hundreds of stories you tell yourself each day, one to which you attached a belief. What is the story you are telling yourself here?

**Question #2:** Is it true?

*Answer:* Yes [ ] No [ ]

Listen to the voice, let your mind ask this question, and just wait for your answer to come. I'm not here to say that your story is neither true nor false. Let the answer come to the surface.

**Question #3:** Can you know for sure that this is 100% true?

*Answer:* Yes [ ] No [ ]

If the answer to question #2 was yes, ask yourself a deeper question. Can you know 100% truly and absolutely for sure that this story is, in fact, true? Can you remember a time that reinforces that this might be false?

**Question #4:** When you think this judgment to be true, how does that make you feel or act?

*Answer:* When I think _____(insert your self-judgement story)_____ to be true, it makes me act/feel _____ (the feeling or action you get when you believe this to be true) _____.

It's important to really go all out on this question, don't hold back and be extremely vulnerable to this question. No one will look over this, and no one will read this. It is for your own record and truly getting out your feelings around this situation.

## The Light

**Question #5:** What might be possible for you in this situation if that thought was, in fact, false, and you were never to have this thought again?

*Answer: If this thought/story was in fact false, it would be possible for me _____ (dive into the possibilities of what your life might be like without this thought) _____. (list the possibilities)*

At this stage, you're like a train running through a tunnel, and you finally catch a glimpse of the light at the end of the tunnel. Take your time, close your eyes if you need to, and let the answer arise into your awareness. The possibilities with you and your thoughts are truly endless. With this story being false, you have so much to offer this world.

**Question #6:** Take a deep breath and picture yourself without that self-judging thought. What does it look like?

*Answer: I see myself _____ (what is the vision you have of yourself without this thought) _____. (list what you see)*

Close your eyes and breath; take your time. Imagine yourself for just a moment being in the shoes of the man you are without being attached to that story. See what you see, hear what you hear, feel what you feel, and enjoy that moment.

## Now Flip It

**Question #7:** What is the thought flipped around?

*Answer: The opposite side of the story is _____ (flip the original story around) _____.*

This is where we start to open up the original story and find its flaws. By now, you have decided that this story is not true. Therefore, holding onto this story starts to become a decision you can make to keep or not. If you want to keep this thought and keep holding onto this story, this is ultimately your choice. Just know that holding onto this will not help you to find liberation.

More often than not, there can be more than one opposite side of the story. For example, in the story 'I should,' one opposite side of the story is 'I shouldn't,' another opposite story is 'I am.'

By flipping the original story, we take all the power and energy out of it and begin to move towards that light we see at the end of the tunnel.

**Question #8:** Now replace 'I' with 'my thinking.' What is this statement?

*Answer: My thinking is* _____ *(insert your original story)* _____.

By replacing 'I,' we are distancing ourselves from this story and bringing in the discovery that it's not us with the story. It's our level of thinking. This is the lift to the light and where you can begin to see that as soon as you change the way you think, you can change your story. The biggest reason you are stuck in this place is that you are stuck in thinking you are stuck in this place. You're not stuck at all; just your thinking is.

**Question #9:** What is the preferred version you wish to adopt now?

*Answer: I choose* _____ *(version of the story)* _____ *because* _____ *(the reason you choose to keep this desired story)* _____.

Here we implant this new adopted story inside your mind by backing it up with the reasons why you choose to keep this story. This is where freedom lies. You now have the power to decide and create a new story around this situation. Nine times out of ten, your original story will completely flip around, allowing you to reach the light and the new possibilities with your now desired version of the story.

**Question #10:** What is your biggest realisation or insight from this Flip?

*Answer: My biggest realisation/insight is _____ (this is your biggest takeaway) _____.*

By asking what your biggest takeaway is, we just cement this desired story further into your mind and awareness so that you can reach the place where you not only believe this new version but also start to act on it consciously and unconsciously.

## Brendon's Example

**Question #1:** What is the self-judgment you are telling yourself?

Answer: *'I should be better at talking to others.'*

**Question #2:** Is it true?

Answer: *'Yes, I always fuck up my conversations. I never know what to say and end up walking about awkwardly'.*

**Question #3:** Can you know for sure that this is true?

Answer: *'No, I can't know for sure. I suppose I've made it in life this far with my level of communication.'*

**Question #4:** When you think this judgment to be true, how does that make you feel or act?

Answer: *'When I think 'I should be better at talking to others', to be honest, it makes me feel like I'm hopeless. I mean, who can't have a normal conversation with someone without getting nervous just talking to them? I feel like a boring person and have nothing to offer anyone. I act in ways that make me avoid any situations where I need to talk to people. I'd rather just accept what I have than ask to change it.'*

**Question #5:** What might be possible for you in this situation if that thought was, in fact, false, and you were never to have this thought again?

Answer: *'If this thought/story were, in fact, false, it would be possible for me to want to talk to people, to know that people will like talking to me and that I have value to add to the conversation. I would be able to get more of what I wanted without shying away from any sort of confrontation. I would be able to actually enjoy conversations instead of wishing for them to hurry up and finish.'*

**Question #6:** Take a deep breath and picture yourself without that self-judging thought. What does it look like?

Answer: *'I see myself as a man. I see myself talking and laughing with ANY-ONE, approaching females and not fucking things up with them. I see myself happy and enjoying life more. I see myself free.'*

**Question #7:** What is the thought flipped around?

Answer: *'The opposite side of the story is that I shouldn't be better at talking to people. I don't need to be better at talking to people. I am better at talking to people.'*

**Question #8:** Now replace 'I' with 'my thinking.' What is this statement?

Answer: *'My thinking should be better at talking to others. My thinking should allow me to be better at talking to others.'*

**Question #9:** What is the preferred version you wish to adopt now?

Answer: *'I choose that I shouldn't need to be better at talking to people because this allows me not to get stressed out if I don't talk to someone better in one situation. I'm not arguing with reality; it just is what it is in my reality.'*

**Question #10:** What is your biggest realisation or insight from this Flip?

Answer: *'My biggest realisation/insight is that my thinking is what has been fucking me up this whole time. If I think I should be better at talking with people, my thoughts influence my actions unknowingly. I am talking to people well. Otherwise, I wouldn't be where I am right now. I can always be better, but no one says I should be.'*

## KEY POINTS

**POINT #1:** It doesn't matter how often we mess up; that's not the problem we have here. It's the stories and lies we get caught up in telling ourselves that are the problem, not the fuck-up itself.

**POINT #2:** These stories become the reason why we live a life of suffering. The suffering that is going on in our minds isn't actually reality.

**POINT #3:** There's a power in the fact that when you put pen to paper or type it out, you are extracting the facts out of the story.

**POINT #4:** If you try to answer these questions internally and in your mind, your mind will shut down any thoughts as quickly as possible when you go against the initial belief.

**POINT #5:** Your mind will fight you every step of the way, not because it's against you, but just because that's what you've led it to believe.

# 12

# PART I: THE SUMMARY

## THE FOUNDATION

*"Anybody can become angry - that is easy, but to be angry with the right person and to the right degree and at the right time and for the right purpose, and in the right way - that is not within everybody's power and is not easy."*

**- Aristotle**

As we arrive at the end of Part I and look back at everything we have discussed so far, it's important to realise that the MMC is not something you just read through once and 'try' to adopt. Firstly, there is no such thing as trying; there is either doing or not doing. Secondly, this is not something that will happen overnight, and it requires commitment. I have faith in you to keep on doing the work and reaping the rewards you will create.

The Code will always be behind you, supporting you as you progress in your journey and guiding you along the way. If you let it go, you will begin to see the results of it being left behind. Think of it as a big lighthouse, just standing in the same location, shining the big bright light over you when you feel you are getting off track. It's the light you need when you are finding yourself in the darkness. If you let go of this, nothing else really matters.

What you should have experienced so far is a new awareness and a new view of your current reality from a fresh pair of eyes. A perspective that might be completely new and maybe even far-fetched for the man you are right now. This is where the power comes with the possibilities. Let's recap.

## The New Awareness

Here, I'll take us back to the *Tao Te Ching* and the idea that what doesn't exist does, in fact, does exist, just not in your current worldview. What might be possible for you now that this new awareness is built? The things that might have seemed impossible for you before are no longer impossible. With that one belief, they become possible.

The new belief allows you to let go of the man you were and transform into the man you can become. The man who is a better provider, producer, partner, and performer. That man is inside of you, you just need to be able to see him, and then he can be woken up and activated.

## 'How Do I Be A Man?'

I don't tell you about the evolution or devolution of man to give you something to blame. It's all about understanding that why we are here is not entirely our fault; it's not something we had control over. But it's also not a reason to sit back, throw your hands in the air and say, 'what's the point?'

The purpose of this is to provide you with the option; you can continue living a mediocre life while blaming the events and actions of old men, or you can use it as fuel to understand that they had the power to change the future. Now you have that exact same power. It all starts with you my brother.

You change a man; you change a family. You change a family; you change a community. You change a community; you change a state. You change a state; you change a country. And if you change a country, you change the world. It all starts with one man; that man is you. The ripple effect is unbelievable.

### Your Father

'Would you be relieved if your father died tomorrow?' 80% of men I've worked with would say yes. If that alone isn't alarming, I don't know what is. Even worse, 90% of my clients have said their fathers would fit into at least one of the following; he was non-existent or never home, he abused him or his family, they hated each other, or he was way too hard/strict. Yes, that's 90%.

I firmly believe that the father is the most influential parent to the child. Yes, the role the mum plays is irreplaceable, absolutely necessary, and cannot be done by the man. A boy looks up to his father to see what a man is supposed to be like, and a girl looks up to him to see what she needs in a potential partner. If you don't consciously give your children a role model to look up to, they will find one, and sometimes that can be the local drug dealer or 'bad boy'.

If you are at war with your father in your head and haven't been able to bring that to peace, that same war can be taken into a war with masculinity itself. Whether you like it or not, your masculinity is based on his. You either reject it, or you adopt it and model it.

There is a danger that you will not become fully mature if you can't reach a place where you can love and respect your father. And by that, I mean deep down, and not just saying it. Whether your father is around or not, coming to terms with him and having an understanding view of him is so important. If you don't, it will haunt you until you do.

## Fatherhood

Boys are so hungry for a male role model that they will look elsewhere if you don't provide it. If you don't consciously be their role model, your sons and daughters will find others to model; you might not like that outcome. If you are a father, this should be one of your #1 roles. Being a father is a commitment, a duty, and a responsibility, and you shouldn't run from it.

## Understand Yourself & Relationship

This is a massive misconception and issue I commonly hear, 'my partner has changed,' 'she's not the same as when we first got together,' or 'we never have fun anymore'. If you begin to work on yourself and improve, the people around you, including your partner, will change. Not because of them, but because of you. If you change, the world around you changes, including your relationship, for better or worse.

Eradicate the thinking that 'women are complicated,' and you'd never be able to understand them. That's bullshit; if that's your thinking, then you're just too lazy to put in the effort. First, before you can even begin to understand anyone else, you need to understand yourself and how to play out your role in a relationship.

## Fortitude & Love

Fortitude is the ability to stand firm, endure and be true to your word. Not take the easy road, not listen to the little bitch voice we all have inside of us and don't hide from things you don't feel like doing. A man with fortitude is mentally strong and someone you can count on. For the right reasons, he would be willing to sacrifice his life.

When a man has mental fortitude and heart, a woman can be his partner, not his mother. Women have the unhealthy tendency to take care of the men in their lives and then resent them, just like men put women on a pedestal and then resent them for being there.

Women were made to nurture, but in healthy relationships, this nurturing must be done in a give-and-take context. They want to serve, yet they also need to be served. They want to give, but they also need to feel that they're receiving. They want to be able to take care of their man, but just as much, they want to feel that he's taking good care of them.

As soon as you begin to notice yourself wanting to give advice, ask her, 'do you want support or answers?' Most times, she doesn't want answers; she wants ears. Not only will you begin to understand her and pick up on the cues, but you're also showing her that you care. Don't stand back, analyse her and give her a diagnosis – aka your opinion – like you're a therapist. Give her your love; show her that you care. Look deeply into her eyes, hold her, smile, and just listen.

## Neediness & Purpose

If a man wants a woman who doesn't want him, he cannot win her over, no matter how hard he tries. His neediness will damage any possible relationship, and he will lose trust and come across as desperate. As soon as she feels his neediness, she feels that he needs her more than she needs him, or she can feel the desperation; she'll lose any attraction to him.

People are attracted to others who are driven and have their 'life on track.' They are ambitious, motivated, hard-working and committed, and most perceive these as attractive traits. When a man has a purpose and knows where he wants to go, others want to be around him.

A woman doesn't really want to be her man's number one, and she might seem to want to be the most important thing in his life. When she feels her man has made her number one, she'll pick up that he's not fully dedicated or directed to his growth. When she becomes a man's highest priority, he'll find his happiness becomes dependent on her. This will make her feel overwhelmed by his neediness.

How committed are you to your current partner and relationship? If it's not 100%, I recommend you ask yourself some of the hard questions as to why it's not 100%.

## Get Real, Raw and Honest

The key to allowing yourself to live by this Code comes down to your ability to get real, be raw, and be honest with who you are and where you want to go. You can shift from living in some fake reality that's made up in your mind and from your own stories to living a true and real life. No more bullshit stories, no more lies and fibs, no longer will you live behind the bars of your own prison or the prison of anyone else's bars.

Before these tools inside the Code were discovered, I couldn't see past the fogged-up glasses with which I was viewing the world. I could not do anything when I was focused so much on the bad and negative. You might be in a similar place, unable to see through your pain and see past that you're hurting. So, nothing even seems remotely possible.

The biggest question I ever asked myself was, 'Is It True?'

I first heard a question in 'The Work' by Bryon Katie, the author of *Loving What Is*. It made me realise that everything in my life was only my version of reality and completely disregarded any sort of facts. Based on this concept, The Flips were born and renamed with the words and terms that support men in liberating themselves from the dark holes we so often fall into. As you go deeper into your stories, you come to find that The Flips you end up doing become somewhat trivial. Because the bigger problems and issues have been worked through, and now it only leaves the little things in your life. This is not a reason to stop. Even the smallest problems need liberation; otherwise, the suppression game will continue.

## KEY POINTS

**POINTS #1:** The Code will always be behind you, supporting you as you progress in your journey and guiding you along the way - Think of it as a big lighthouse.

**POINTS #2:** The Tao Te Ching - what doesn't exist does, in fact, does exist, just not in your current worldview. Things that might have seemed impossible for you before are no longer impossible.

**POINTS #3:** The man who is a better provider, producer, partner, and performer is inside of you, you just need to be able to see him, and then he can be woken up and activated.

**POINTS #4:** You can continue living a mediocre life while blaming the events and actions of old men, or you can use it as fuel to understand that they had the power to change the future. Now you have that exact same power.

**POINTS #5:** The key to allowing yourself to live by this Code comes down to your ability to get real, be raw, and be honest with who you are and where you want to go.

# 13

# PART II: THE OVERVIEW

## THE 5 PILLARS

*"There is a sacredness in tears. They are not the mark of weakness, but of power. They speak more eloquently than ten thousand tongues. They are the messengers of overwhelming grief, of deep contrition, and of unspeakable love."*
**- Washington Irving**

In the teachings of the ancient Toltec philosophy, we are not at war with anyone else outside of ourselves. The war is won and lost inside ourselves and starts with the societal and parental programming our minds have been exposed to. The path to personal freedom is hard to master, but through Toltec wisdom, the avenue to a new experience of freedom, true happiness, and love becomes possible.

The Toltec people were known throughout the south of Mexico as 'women and men of knowledge'. They resided in the ancient city of pyramids outside Mexico City, known as the place where 'Man Becomes God.'

I was first introduced to the Toltecs and the four agreements by Don Miguel Ruiz and his book *The 4 Agreements*[24]. He spoke about these agreements that could lead to personal freedom. This seemed impossible to me at the time. All I wanted was to be free and have this level of personal freedom that I kept hearing about, but I just could not find it. And nobody could tell me where it was.

## Your Current Agreements

I can tell you now that you already have a list of agreements you live by. You have unknowingly agreed to them as soon as you believed them to be true. There was no choice for you to speak the English language. You weren't able to choose your religion or even your moral values. They were all in place before you were born. There was never an opportunity to consciously choose what to believe or what not to believe. These agreements were passed on to us by the adults around us.

As we age, we start to question these agreements and question these beliefs. After all, they are not ours to begin with. But as most men have been taught to do, we do not take a stand. We succumb to the sedation game once again and decide that we 'cannot do anything or take a stand' as it's not accepted or politically correct to have a different worldview. To that, I give it a big middle finger.

Before becoming aware of the agreements and the beliefs associated with them, I unknowingly had been passed the following agreements:

1. Do not tell anyone how you feel

2. Conflict is 'bad' and not 'socially acceptable'

3. Speaking the truth doesn't mean shit

4. Do not speak out of turn or take a stand for something seen as 'different.'

5. Just keep going and don't complain

And not to mention all the money and scarcity agreements.

The same can be seen when you dive deeper to expose the agreements of the men I've coached. These same agreements, which I previously believed, are becoming more and more prevalent amongst other men. In that case, the question must be asked where exactly these distorted world views are coming from.

## Letting Go of the Old

To be able to adopt new agreements, you must first let go of current ones. This may be the hardest part of your journey to becoming a king. As a matter of fact, the agreements you are holding onto right now are the ones that have made you into the man you are today. In some ways, it's beautiful; in others, it's destroying you. It's not for me to say which is the case for you, but it leads me to ask the question, 'Is your life working?'

If you answer yes, then the agreements you currently have are working, and you can continue to live like that. But if you answer no, I guess your life isn't working to the fullest extent. Otherwise, you probably wouldn't be reading this. If that is the case, you are only left with one option: to adopt new agreements. What allows you to adopt these new agreements is establishing a new foundation on top of the Five Pillars.

## The New Foundation

There is no surprise that we need to build a solid foundation before we begin to transform our lives. Although, this is no normal foundation, and this isn't just a flat surface to build on. We are driving 5 strong pillars down into the ground that will support you in any situation, challenge, adversity or difficulty. The strongest men have the strongest foundation.

It was a long time before all 5 Pillars were discovered. At first, it was just one, then bit by bit, as my real-life results proved these to work, I added in the next one I felt was missing. I was and still am now, always asking myself, 'what can I add to make this better,' and the same was true for my life. That question was the same one I had asked myself every day for two years straight, and I still have the three notebooks I used then. 'What can I add to make my life better?'

If you are not adding to your life, you are losing. If you are not improving, you are going backwards. If you are not growing, you are dying. It's that simple. It's not hard, and it's not complicated; it's a fact. If staying the same and just 'floating' through life is what you're aiming for, that's totally cool. But you probably don't need to read on any further. On the other hand, if you are striving for self-mastery, to be great, to be the best you can be, and to not settle for average, these Pillars are essential to your progress.

## The Framework

As we go through this second part of the book, I'm giving you the framework and overview of the 5 Pillars. I'm not telling you exactly what you need to do or how you must live your life. Instead, I want to give you the framework so you can make it fit into your current situation. Just note that as you grow and change, so will your life and how you view this framework. It will 100% change.

These Pillars have developed over 6 years of questioning myself, questioning reality and what's 'normal.' From the books, courses, programs, seminars, events, spiritual awakenings and experiences, I finally discovered these 5 Pillars designed to: 1. Win the internal war with yourself, 2. Be the best for everyone around you, 3. Guide you to personal freedom.

## KEY POINTS

**POINT #1:** Toltec philosophy - we are not at war with anyone else outside of ourselves. The war is won and lost inside ourselves and starts with the societal and parental programming our minds have been exposed to.

**POINT #2:** You already have a list of agreements you live by. You have unknowingly agreed to them as soon as you believed them to be true.

**POINT #3:** To be able to adopt new agreements, you must first let go of current ones. This may be the hardest part of your journey to becoming a king.

**POINT #4:** If you are not adding to your life, you are losing. If you are not improving, you are going backwards. If you are not growing, you are dying. It's that simple. It's not hard, and it's not complicated; it's a fact.

**POINT #5:** These 5 Pillars are designed to;

1. Win the internal war with yourself,
2. Be the best for everyone around you,
3. Guide you to personal freedom.

# 14

# THE FIRST PILLAR

## DO YOUR BEST

*"I believe that in life, you have to give things your best shot, do your best. You have to focus on what needs to be done, do the right thing, not the popular thing."*
**- David Cameron**

This is the first of the Pillars, and it's the one that opens the gates to ingrain the next four pillars into habits. Think of it as the glue that links this foundation together. Do your best in every situation and in everything you do. To quantify this to a new level, when you adopt the Daily 8 into your life, your best will become something you had never thought possible. Don't worry; we'll discuss the Daily 8 in Part IV.

Just remember that your best isn't always the highest you can do. The times you are fully alert and energised will produce higher results than when you are tired and exhausted. At the same time, you can still do your best in each situation. Your best will be better when you feel great as opposed to you feeling shitty or whether you are feeling cheerful and happy or pissed off, angry and jealous.

## Play The Long Game

Regardless of the results you are producing, just keep doing your best. If you try to do any more than your best, you will expend too much effort and energy that is not needed. In the end, and in these situations, your best will never be good enough. This is not a sprint; it's a marathon. Yer, I know you've heard that before, but it's true. Life is full of instant gratification, and everyone what's everything right now. After Pay, Zip Pay, Credit Cards and personal loans are all examples. These can be very useful resources when used wisely, but most of the time, they are not. So don't max out your limit on one day; just do the best you can for that individual day.

## Quality Over Quantity

As you go through each day, you'll discover that this saying, quality over quantity, will run true when you always do your best. Doing your best will result in you living your life fully and intensely. You'll be productive, and you'll be good to yourself. You'll be happy and give yourself to your family, friends, and community.

A strange thing happens when you start to do your best. You start to accept yourself for who you are, the mistakes you make, and the results you produce. You'll start to kill excuses and eradicate any sign of the bitch voice trying to talk you out of doing things. Doing your best leaves you with no regrets. When you do your best, all the time, you cannot regret that. If you look back and regret something, that's a good sign because it means you have grown. If you were to look back and notice what you did and think nothing was wrong with it, you haven't grown. Therefore, regret is a good thing. It's showing you how you can improve. We really only learn from our mistakes and the things we do wrong. Embrace it. Learn from it. Grow from it.

## Are You Doing Your Best?

Nowadays, I have this little voice constantly questioning me. If I'm writing, it says, 'are you doing your best?' if I'm at the gym, 'are you doing your best?' if I'm spending time with family and friends, 'are you doing your best?' if I'm working, 'are you doing your best?'.

This is what happens when you change your internal dialogue and develop mental strength and emotional intelligence, which is my goal for you in the program. I say program because it is. It isn't just a book you read; it's a program you complete and continue to live by.

## The Boss vs The Bitch

As Andy Frisella describes it in his book *75 HARD*, 'every day...there is an epic battle going on inside you. It's the battle between two voices in your head. I call them The Boss Voice and The Bitch Voice.'[25] When you commit to always doing the best you can in the current moment, you'll drown out the bitch voice. Things will get easier, you'll get mentally stronger, you'll get better, you'll do more, and your confidence and self-esteem will grow exponentially. Worth the payoff, right?

Whether you are sick, tired or worn out, none of that makes any difference if you always do the best you can at the time. There is no way you can judge yourself if that's what you do. Without judgement, there's no way you will be able to suffer from feeling guilt, blaming or punishing yourself.

## Break The Spell

If you continually do your best, you will break the spell you have been under. The spell of negativity and lower vibrational emotions. When you're not living in those lower emotions, you can spend more time at the higher vibration of happiness, joy and love. If you know about the Law of Attraction, this happens at the higher frequencies.

An amazing thing begins to happen when you commit to always doing your best; you take action. There is no procrastination or putting things off, and you take action because you love it. Action brings results, and results bring further action; it's a winning cycle. When you do it because you love it, there's no need for a reward. Most people do the complete opposite.

## Expecting No Rewards

If you only take action when expecting some sort of reward, you'll never enjoy what you're doing. You're never going to enjoy or even want to take action. You won't ever do your best when you don't enjoy it, and you'll do only the bare minimum you need to do to get by. The perfect example of this is when people go to work every day, only thinking about the paycheck they'll get on payday. I would go as far as saying most people are like this.

I used to be exactly the same, and look where I nearly ended up: being buried by my parents. Working in a FIFO job just for the money, basically wishing my life away until I could get onto my 7 days off. I was working for the reward, and as a result, I resisted work and only did what I needed to do to pass the time.

This is the same for so many men; they can hardly wait for the week-end so they can take time off. Again, working for the reward, working for the paycheck. This leads men to begin avoiding action and work becomes more difficult. When it's difficult, and they don't want to do it, they will never do their best.

This is when work becomes something they 'have to' do, not because they like to. Currently, I'm working anywhere from 60-90hrs a week. I'm not saying this for any other reason than I love what I do, and I never feel like I have to. Taking action is never an issue. The same will be true for you, whether it's your own business or you're an employee. Why not make the most of what you do because we spend soo much of our lives doing it.

When you see work as something you need to do only because you have to pay the rent, support your family, or put food on the table, it will always become a drag. This will make you frustrated and maybe even curse your boss. More times than not, when you receive your pay, you'll still be unhappy.

So now you've got your pay which you're unhappy about, and you have 1 or 2 days to rest on your weekend. What do many men want to do, and what do they do? They try to escape. They get drunk because they don't like themselves, and they don't like their life. We have so many ways we hurt ourselves when we are not happy within or if we don't like ourselves. When you're truly happy and love yourself, there's no need to escape or cause pain to yourself.

If we flip this over, by taking action and doing your best, for no other reason than because you can and want to, without expecting a reward or payback. You will no longer find things to be a hassle and will begin to enjoy every action you take.

Although others might think this is the least important Pillar, this 'do your best' mantra has been one of the biggest accelerators in my life. If you take one thing from this book, I urge you to try it out for 30 days and see what happens. I highly doubt that you will not want to continue living true to this Pillar.

## KEY POINTS

**POINT #1:** Do your best in every situation and in everything you do.

**POINT #2:** Remember that your best isn't always the highest you can do. The times you are fully alert and energised will produce higher results than when you are tired and exhausted.

**POINT #3:** Regardless of the results you are producing, just keep doing your best.

**POINT #4:** You'll start to accept yourself for who you are, the mistakes you make, and the results you produce. You'll start to kill excuses and eradicate any sign of the bitch voice trying to talk you out of doing things.

**POINT #5:** If you continually do your best, you will break the spell you have been under. The spell of negativity and lower vibrational emotions.

**POINT #6:** Try it out for 30 days and see what happens.

# 15

## THE SECOND PILLAR

### USE YOUR WORD WISELY

*"It's not only moving that creates new starting points. Sometimes all it takes is a subtle shift in perspective, an opening of the mind, an intentional pause and reset, or a new route to start to see new options and new possibilities."*
## - Kristin Armstrong

Arguably this pillar will be the hardest for most men to adopt and live by. It is simple but very powerful. Since your thoughts and words represent your choices, learning how to think and speak to intentionally create what you desire can be of great value to your life.

Your word is the most powerful tool that you have as a human being. Depending on how you use your word, it can create the life of your dreams, or it can destroy the world underneath you. It can set you free or enslave you more than you ever thought possible.

To demonstrate just how powerful your word is and to understand that just one word can either change a life or destroy millions of lives. Look at the Founding Fathers of America and the Declaration of Independence that came from their word. Consider Hitler in Germany, who manipulated a whole country by using his word in speeches. Pol Pot began the Khmer Rouge with his word, and nearly every man who has started some sort of revolution, whether for good or bad, all began with their word.

The way that you use your word is about more than just telling the truth. Yes, you can tell yourself a lie that you might be stupid, which is using the word against you. But it gets quantified at a new level. If I were to see someone in the street and call them stupid, it would seem like I'm using the word against them. But in reality, I'm actually using the word against myself. That person will hate me for saying that, and the fact that that person hates me is not good for me. So really, my word would be working against me.

### Your Projection

Everything in your life is a projection of yourself. So whenever you use your word against someone else, and if they are your projection of you, you can see why it's hurting you. Gandhi said, 'Be the change you wish to see in the world.'[26] When you think about this to a deeper level, your projection of the world is how you want to see it. So when you change, your projection changes and the change you wish to see in the world will happen.

When you get angry, frustrated, or pissed off with the people around you, what you are really getting angry at is your own projection. All anger is self-anger, and it's never the thing that makes you angry; it's your perception of it. It's never them; it's always you. This might be a hard concept to grasp, and that's why I've developed The Flips; to help you deal with this.

If you love yourself, your love will be expressed in your interactions with others, and your action will produce a like-for-like reaction. If you insult someone, they will insult you back. If you show love to someone, they will show love back to you. If you show gratitude towards someone, they will show gratitude towards you. If you are selfish with someone, they will be selfish back. Therefore, if you use your word against someone, they will use it back on you, in the same way or in a different form.

### Words Against Yourself

We talk to ourselves constantly, and unfortunately, most of the time we say things like, 'I'm not happy with myself. I look terrible. I'm getting old. I'm losing my hair. I can't do X. I'm useless. I'm not good enough. I'm never going to get there.' See how often we use our own words against ourselves? When you understand your words and what they can do, you'll begin to see many changes in your life. Changes first with how you deal with yourself and then how you deal with others.

A few years back, I watched a documentary on YouTube called 'What The Bleep.'[27] There was a part of the film where they spoke about how thoughts and words actually change the structure of water. One study showed the structure of the water under a microscope that had been blessed by a Buddhist Monk. Blessed by thoughts and words. They compared the blessed water with unblessed water from the same tap, and the results were amazing. It was like the blessed water had turned into crystals.

A second study had a water bottle with words taped on the side. Nothing else was done to the water, literally the words just written on the bottle. One said thank you, and the other said hate. As you could have guessed, the structure was completely different, and I was shocked to see how 'bad' the hate bottle looked. You might think this is BS until you see it. Go check it out on YouTube and see for yourself.

The point I want to make here is this; look at the effect those words and thoughts had on the bottles of water. Our bodies are made up of 60-70% water. So imagine what your thoughts are doing to you. When you use your words against yourself, you are potentially changing the structure of the water inside your body.

## Words For Yourself

Use your word to start breaking all those little beliefs that make you suffer on a daily basis. Tell yourself how great you are, how wonderful you are, and how grateful you are towards yourself. When you can lock down this Pillar and master your words and thoughts, not only will you learn to not use your words against yourself, but others won't be able to use their words on you. They won't be able to get past your gatekeeper, and you'll just brush them off.

That is the definition of mental toughness. Being able to stand tall and not let what anyone else is saying affect you in any way. It must start with you. If you're still using your words against yourself, others will also be used against you. But when you are not, this same will be true for the words of others.

If I can break my old beliefs and agreements by first using the power of the word on myself, then you can too. Using your words wisely can lead you to be free, have massive success, and live in abundance.

## <u>KEY POINTS</u>

**POINT #1:** Learning how to think and speak to intentionally create what you desire can be of great value to your life.

**POINT #2:** Depending on how you use your word, it can create the life of your dreams, or it can destroy the world underneath you. It can set you free or enslave you more than you ever thought possible.

**POINT #3:** Everything in your life is a projection of yourself.

**POINT #4:** Gandhi said, 'Be the change you wish to see in the world.' When you think about this to a deeper level, your projection of the world is how you want to see it. So when you change, your projection changes and the change you wish to see in the world will happen.

**POINT #5:** When you can lock down this Pillar and master your words and thoughts, not only will you learn to not use your words against yourself, but others won't be able to use their words on you.

# 16

## THE THIRD PILLAR

### RESPECT OTHERS MODEL OF THE WORLD

*"Respect for ourselves guides our morals, respect for others guides our manners."*
- **Laurence Sterne**

The Third Pillar is related to the second; *respect others' model of the world.* Nothing others say or do directly results from you. It's a projection of their own reality, fantasy, and model of the world. Each and every one of us lives inside our reality in our 24-hour dreams or fantasy. Yes, we dream with our eyes open and with our eyes closed. Most men are already walking around asleep all the time, but it's not their fault; they just haven't been taught or shown how to become awake.

At the point when you are unshakable to the opinions and actions of others, and nothing they can say will affect you, you will never be the casualty of unnecessary suffering. When you accept something personally, you assume that they know what's happening inside your world and that their view is your reality as well as theirs. Who has the power in this situation? Who has YOUR power in this situation? Not you!

If you allow yourself to be affected by others' opinions, their judgements or even if they bother you in the slightest, they have your power. You are allowing them to use your power against you.

## Right vs Wrong

Whether something is right or wrong is all based on perception. What's right for you might be wrong for someone else, and what's right for them might be wrong for you. Neither is right or wrong; it's based on perception and the individual worldview. Killing someone in the street is murder, but killing someone like Osama bin Laden is celebrated. Both are murder, just different perspectives. In that same situation but on the opposing side, the World Trade Center attacks were celebrated by Islamic extremists, but Osama's death was bad. It all depends on the model of the world. Look, I'm not saying what happened was right in my model of the world either; this is just an example to show you the different models of the world.

When you can respect others' models of the world, you can then understand why people do the things they do. You will begin to understand why they say and do the things they do, and more importantly, the things they do won't affect you. It gives you the upper hand and a heightened level of awareness of the people around you.

People will see you how they want to see you with whatever is happening inside them. If someone suppresses their anger or confidence, they will see others as over-angry, overconfident, or cocky. By the way, a lack of confidence is a suppression of confidence. We are all born fully confident; it just gets a hit along the way. So unconsciously, we've learnt to suppress our confidence to protect ourselves.

What others think about you isn't actually what you are like, and it's just their view of you from the model they have constructed in their mind. This is why two people can see the exact same event or situation and respond completely differently.

## Unpacking The Past

I had a client, let's call him Bob, who came to me wanting to improve himself after an incident at home with his wife. This was the moment that woke him up. He was asleep before this happened, so it needed to happen for Bob to wake up. Sometimes life will throw you problems to force you to wake up if you haven't consciously decided to wake up. And if you don't wake up that time, it will continue throwing them until you do.

Bob had a few things going on, but the thing I want to discuss here is an incident where he had no idea what happened, and it ended up with him getting taken away by the police. To keep the story short, Bob's 8-year-old daughter was hitting her 6-year-old brother over the head with their pet guinea pig. Bob ran out and stopped the fight, smacked his daughter on the bum, and it was all over. That was until his wife ran out and started yelling at Bob and saying he was kicking her. Anyway, a few days later, Bob got arrested. His wife had told the police that he had kicked the daughter 7 times with steel cap boots.

In our first session with Bob, I asked him about this incident. He said nothing like that happened and didn't understand why his wife would say something like this. Turns out Bob told me that she had a very aggressive father that actually kicked her 7 times as a girl when she was putting her pet rabbit away. This got my attention. I asked a few more questions, and he continued to tell me about all the times she would get angry at him. I got a list of all the things and asked him, 'who does this person sound like?' Bob said that's exactly what his wife said her dad was like.

So Bob's wife had a switch flick in these situations that caused her to see Bob as her father, and she'd be back reliving her childhood. He then started to see things from her model of the world. They spoke about this, she understood, and I actually ended up working with her for a few sessions, and we cleared this childhood trauma up with her. Now they are back living together, and their relationship has never been better. This is the power of understanding and respecting someone else's model of the world.

### It's Not Personal

If someone insults you directly or when a situation seems so personal, it doesn't have anything to do with you. What others say, what others do, and the opinions of others are all a direct response to their belief system and agreements inside their own mind, not yours.

This can be a hard concept to grasp. When you have someone directly in your face saying, 'You're bloody hopeless,' it's hard to accept that what they are saying has *nothing* to do with you. When you receive the statement 'You're bloody hopeless,' instead of accepting it and believing it to be about 'me,' you ask yourself that little question, can I really know that is 100% true? Am I 100% sure that I'm hopeless? From this, you come to realise that what they're saying is not your belief at all. If you do take on their belief, you have then accepted and agreed it to be true, and their word has influenced you. Not only that, but they have your power. If you let someone or something get to you, you have given your power to them.

Many believe this way of living is selfish, but in fact, it's the complete opposite. If you take something personally, you get offended and try to counteract by defending your beliefs. Something that might be such a small deal can be blown out of proportion due to the need to be right and everyone else wrong. This is selfish behaviour.

When you live with the thought of 'whatever you think about me is not important to me, so I don't care what you think about me,' you will become free. If people say to me, 'Brendon, you are the best,' I don't take it personally, nor do I take it personally when they say, 'Brendon, you suck.' The only thing that really matters is how you think about yourself.

The path to personal freedom is not accepting others' opinions of you. If you receive a personal comment that hits you hard or provokes a reaction in you, that is something you must inquire about within yourself before accepting another's opinion. If someone says something that gets to me, all I ask is, why did that hurt me so much? What in that statement is triggering my insecurities? What is this person showing me that I need to work on within myself? This is a completely different way of looking at things and will lead to personal freedom.

## KEY POINTS

**POINT#1:** Nothing others say or do directly results from you. It's a projection of their own reality, fantasy, and model of the world.

**POINT#2:** When you accept something personally, you assume that they know what's happening inside your world and that their view is your reality as well as theirs.

**POINT#3:** When you can respect others' models of the world, you can then understand why people do and say the things they do. More importantly, the things they do won't affect you.

**POINT#4:** Personal freedom is not accepting others' opinions of you. If you receive a personal comment that hits you hard or provokes a reaction in you, that is something you must inquire about within yourself before accepting another's opinion.

**POINT#5:** This is a completely different way of looking at things and will lead to personal freedom.

# 17

# THE FORTH PILLAR

## ASSUME NOTHING

*"Because your own strength is unequal
to the task, do not assume that it is
beyond the powers of man; but if
anything is within the powers and
province of man, believe that it is
within your own compass also."*
### - Marcus Aurelius

As a human race, we tend to make assumptions about everything. Take a moment to consider the truth inside this. Every bit of unhappiness and trouble you have experienced in your life comes from making assumptions and accepting someone else's reality. Because we are afraid to ask people to clarify in order to find out the truth, we enter into a cycle of assumptions. We are afraid to ask the hard questions we know we should be asking, fearing the answer we might not want to hear.

From not knowing the answer and a lack of clarification, we make an assumption of what we believe to be true. This leads us to defend our assumptions to make out another person is wrong; your assumptions set you up to do nothing but suffer. Our assumptions generally become our opinions. How often do you hear or see people arguing their opinions non-stop, sometimes for days or weeks, especially in relationships? Would this happen if they didn't assume?

We only see what we want to see, hear what we want to hear, and believe what we want to believe. To end up only perceiving the bits we want to perceive and, on the whole, not seeing them the way they are. So as soon as you form an assumption or opinion, you'll start searching for 'evidence' to back that up. What you search for is what you find, and you'll conveniently delete everything else.

An example of this is, say you walk into the house to greet your partner, only for her to hear or see you and walk away. You make the assumption that she knows you are home: she heard you, and she saw you. You, therefore, also assume that you must have done something wrong because she is ignoring you. But in reality, she might not have seen or heard you at all. As I said earlier, we only take in what we want to. Her mind could have completely blocked you from even being there, not because she didn't want to see or acknowledge you, but because she had other things at the front of her mind at that time.

### Programmed To Be Negative

How often have you finished a conversation with someone, only to think, 'What did they mean by that?'. By doing this, you make your own assumption of what they meant without asking what they actually meant. Our minds are designed to keep us safe and look for threats and problems, so we tend to make the least desired assumption and run with it. Our minds are literally designed to look for negatives, not to mention the negative programming we receive along the way.

Most of us have received this negative programming from parents, teachers and carers. During the first 18 years of our lives, if we grew up in fairly average, reasonably positive homes, we were told 'no', or what we could not do, more than 148,000 times.[28] That's over 8,000 times a year. This is why you might also seem to be negative. Again, it's no one's fault; it's just what happens. You can see why we tend to assume the worse in certain situations.

Most of us also assume that everyone sees life exactly the same way we do. We tend to think that others think the same as we think, see life the same as we see life, feel the same as we feel, criticise the same as we criticise, and shame the same as we shame. This is why it takes so long for people to warm up around others and fear being 'ourselves.' We think everyone else will criticise us, shame us, victimise us, and blame us as we do to ourselves. Before they even have the chance to reject us, we have already rejected ourselves.

This is why so many men fail in dating and relationships. Instead of just asking, we make assumptions that stuff our lives and thoughts. You believe an assumption to be true, so you start to take action on that assumption being true, only for it not to be true. But you have come too far with your assumption that was never true in the first place.

## Communication Is Key

We often think we don't have to communicate what we want to our partners, assuming they already know. We assume they will do what we want, and we assume that they know us well enough to know. If they don't, we feel unwanted and unloved and say, 'You should have known.' Imagine the day you stop making assumptions about everyone in your life. Your communication will change completely, you won't constantly search for the negatives, and your relationships will no longer suffer from your mistaken assumptions.

To stop making these assumptions, you can do one simple thing: ASK! Ask questions if you don't understand or aren't 100% clear. So many men are too scared to ask questions because of many reasons. Whether it be because they are scared of looking dumb or stupid, not wanting to seem like they weren't listening or even worse, not wanting to know the truth. Have the courage to ask questions, even if they are hard. Don't not ask a question because you are scared of the answer; this will lead to a hard and lacking life. You didn't come here to live an average or lacking life.

It's better for you to ask than it is to make an assumption. I can tell you now that the day you stop assuming is the day you will begin to communicate clearly and cleanly. The day you stop assuming is also the day you liberate yourself from the emotional prison you have succumbed to. With clear communication, all of your relationships will change. Put simply, it would be, this is what I want; this is what you want. If everyone communicated this way, the number of wars, violence and misunderstandings would be greatly reduced.

## Action

Just like anything, information is useless by itself. It's only useful when you take action. Learning how to read is useless unless you do the action of reading. Understanding how to lose weight or build muscle is useless until you put it into action. Learning how to invest will not make you money until you put it into action. The same is true with this. If you don't put it into action, nothing will ever change.

This will be unfamiliar at first, and it seems a lot easier said than done because we often do the exact opposite. Most of the time, we do these unconsciously, so we don't realise we are doing them. Once you notice the things you do unconsciously, you can begin to consciously change them. This is the art of waking up and becoming awakened.

Action equals change. When you take consistent action, you'll build new habits and strengthen your ability to do them unconsciously. This is where the magic happens. Taking an unwanted unconscious behaviour, becoming conscious of it, taking conscious action to change it, and then the new behaviour becomes unconscious again. Un-desired unconscious to conscious to desired unconscious. Asleep to Aware to Awakened.

So again, the Forth Pillar – *Assume Nothing*

## KEY POINTS

**POINT #1:** Every bit of unhappiness and trouble you have experienced in your life comes from making assumptions and accepting someone else's reality.

**POINT #2:** We are afraid to ask the hard questions we know we should be asking, fearing the answer we might not want to hear.

**POINT #3:** We only see what we want to see, hear what we want to hear, and believe what we want to believe. To end up only perceiving the bits we want to perceive and, on the whole, not seeing them the way they are.

**POINT #4:** What you search for is what you find, and you'll conveniently delete everything else.

**POINT #5:** Our minds are designed to keep us safe and look for threats and problems, so we tend to make the least desired assumption and run with it.

**POINT #6:** During the first 18 years of our lives, we were told 'no', or what we could not do, more than 148,000 times.

**POINT #7:** Imagine the day you stop making assumptions about everyone in your life.

**POINT #8:** This is where the magic happens, taking an unwanted unconscious behaviour, becoming conscious of it, taking conscious action to change it, and then the new behaviour becomes unconscious again.

# 18

# THE FIFTH PILLAR

## HIGH EXPECTATIONS, DETACHED OUTCOMES

*"Let us be about setting high standards for life, love, creativity, and wisdom. If our expectations in these areas are low, we are not likely to experience wellness. Setting high standards makes every day and every decade worth looking forward to."*

**- Greg Anderson**

If you speak to many life coaches, a lot of them will say that releasing your expectations will lead to happiness. I agree with this in some ways, and I have said before that expectations can kill your happiness, but this is only one side of the equation. On one side, if we don't have expectations, we'll never get anywhere. On the other, if our expectations are too high and we don't reach them, it can cause a lot of stress, worry and unhappiness. So how do we counteract this?

In 2018 I sat in a 5-day online seminar run by a life coach out of Brisbane; well, I think that's what he called himself. I'm not going to mention his name here as he did have a few good things to say. He went on to explain his concept on expectations. I say his concept because that's what he was teaching, his viewpoint of expectations. It's not right or wrong, just different, and I'm going to tell you about my experience with this and why it might not be best for you.

One of the first things he said that got my attention was that 'if we hold high expectations and fail, we'll never be able to live a fully fulfilling life. When you can drop your expectations of yourself and others, you will be able to find the happiness you desire.' That's not exactly what he said, but it's as close as I can recall.

So now I had this concept that my expectations determined my happiness, and the way to become happy was to drop them. Well, according to old mate and I agreed to that at first. For the next few months, that's what I did. I dropped my expectations of myself and others around me. Whenever something happened that didn't make me happy, I put it down to my expectations and moved on.

I'm not going to lie; it worked at first. Every time I did something that didn't go the way I wanted, I thought maybe I expected too much and let myself off the hook. If someone let me down, I thought maybe I expected too much from them and let them off the hook. If I didn't make a goal, I thought it was ok because my expectations must have been too high.

Suddenly, one day after reflecting over the last few months, it hit me. I had become a fucking pushover. I was letting people walk over me. I was letting myself off the hook and wasn't getting anywhere. Maybe I got this concept wrong in relation to what he was trying to teach, but I'd become a pussy.

This whole concept of letting go of expectations didn't work for me, and I can see it everywhere. It seems like many men don't have high enough expectations in their roles as fathers and husbands or, more importantly, within themselves. Accountability and self-accountability are nonexistent.

## Why Expectations Can Cause Us Pain

When our reality doesn't match our expectations, we can become discouraged and begin to suffer. So many of us have our age attached as the timeframe we expect to have achieved certain milestones. If we fail to hit it by then, we feel the pain and unhappiness it causes. Maybe it's an age you expected to be married, start a family, reach a certain level in your career or reach a certain financial level. Maybe you expect other people to always be kind, respectful and trustworthy.

These are our beliefs about how life 'should' turn out. When reality doesn't live up to these beliefs, we tend to blame our circumstances, ourselves and other people for our disappointment. This gives you a fair point about expectations, but as I mentioned earlier, no one would ever achieve anything if we dropped all expectations.

## The New Model

Now I want to pivot to a new model of expectations. I believe we all should have expectations and strive to live up to them. In this new model, the expectations drive the outcome, not your happiness. Your happiness is determined by being content in your inner world, and you don't let these expectations determine your happiness.

When you approach life through this lens, you'll begin to push your personal growth along much faster, and the things you don't achieve will be a new chance for growth. Life is one big lesson; we are forever doing and trying new things. It still surprises me why so many of us beat ourselves up for not achieving things we've never done before. To go through life and achieve everything you want in the desired time-frame is unrealistic. I'm not sure anyone on this planet has done that. So why do we get down on ourselves for it?

Life is a lesson, and we learn best from our mistakes. So if you don't achieve a target that you'd like to achieve – aka a mistake – you must learn from it and grow. If you look back and dwell on it, regret any decisions or focus on how you failed, you will be upset. As mentioned earlier, this is allowing your expectations to determine your happiness.

If you have an expectation that hasn't been met, whether by you or someone else, you must reflect and reassess. Looking at your mistakes or failures through this lens is a complete perspective shift. You are reflecting on what went well, what didn't go so well and what you can do better in the future. By doing this, you are taking control and allowing yourself to be the one who determines any future outcomes.

## Control

First, we must start by eliminating the belief that our life results from circumstances beyond our control. Reflecting and growing from these unmet expectations means you accept responsibility for your emotions, actions and life. Once you accept that you are the only person you can control, you'll stop expecting others to live up to an imaginary ideal.

I worked with a client, let's call him Joe, about 6 months ago as he was going through a 'separation.' I say separation in quotation marks as either Joe or his wife didn't really know what they wanted. One minute they wanted to get back together; the next it was over, which went on for a few weeks. One of the biggest expectations holding him there was the idea of an unbroken family. Joe grew up in a broken family and swore to himself that he wouldn't have one.

This expectation of his unbroken family was tied directly to his happiness. This is why it rocked him so much when it came tumbling down. As we dug a bit deeper, it turned out Joe had been checked out for over 3 years, but this expectation of the perfect family drove him to want to work things out with her. I guided him through a few processes, and he soon realised what went wrong in the relationship, where he wasn't the husband or father he needed to be, and how he could do better in the future.

A physical shift in Joe's physiology occurred, and I knew we were done. He'd released the expectation of this perfect family and could now see the whole relationship as a new experience for growth. Joe had let go of the outcome. The following weeks after this, his business doubled its profits, his relationship with his children improved, and he even met an amazing woman. As I've said before, when you change, the world around you changes; this is another example of this.

## Detach The Outcome

Joe had the expectation of a perfect family that had served him for so long. It was a driving force, and it was useful. Would I want him to not have that expectation? That expectation kept his marriage together for 15 years, and they had 2 beautiful kids. If he didn't, he probably would have been in and out of relationships for the whole 15 years. So expectations are good. They are needed. They are what drive you to success.

Healthy expectations are ones where you can detach from the outcome, and this is the new model I'm showing you here. Don't let your dreams and aspirations die because you fear your expectations will affect your happiness. Would you rather attempt to reach your goals and only get halfway, or not attempt them at all? I know what I'd rather do.

Let's use the example that you had an expectation of being married and having kids by a certain age. If you didn't have this expectation, you probably wouldn't put much or any effort into this. Even though you had this expectation, unfortunately, you didn't make it. So you've hit the expected age, the target hasn't been achieved and now what? First, we look at the facts. Am I where I want to be? No. Ok, cool, so let's reflect. Where have I gone wrong over the last 5 years? What could I have done differently? Have I put 100% effort into this? What can I improve for the future? Don't stop here; keep asking questions, getting insights and learning from where you went wrong. This gives you data for you to grow and improve.

This is detaching the outcome from your expectation and, ultimately, your happiness. It may take some time to get the hang of it, and it's a much better way to move forward to hit the targets in your life than sitting back and having no expectations.

## KEY POINTS

**POINT #1:** On one side, if we don't have expectations, we'll never get anywhere. On the other, if our expectations are too high and we don't reach them, it can cause a lot of stress, worry and unhappiness.

**POINT #2:** It seems like many men don't have high enough expectations in their roles as fathers and husbands or, more importantly, within themselves. Accountability and self-accountability are nonexistent.

**POINT #3:** The New Model

- Expectations drive the outcome, not your happiness. Your happiness is determined by being content in your inner world, and you don't let these expectations determine your happiness.

**POINT #4:** Life is one big lesson; we are forever doing and trying new things, yet so many of us beat ourselves up for not achieving things we've never done before.

**POINT #5:** We learn best from our mistakes. So if you don't achieve a target that you'd like to achieve – aka a mistake – you must learn from it and grow.

**POINT #6:** Healthy expectations are ones where you can detach from the outcome.

**POINT #7:** Don't let your dreams and aspirations die because you fear your expectations will affect your happiness.

# 19

# PART II: THE SUMMARY

## THE 5 PILLARS

*"The carrying power of a bridge is not the average strength of the pillars, but the strength of the weakest pillar."*
**- Zygmunt Bauman**

**If You Fall, Get Back Up**

The last thing I want to cover inside this section is that it doesn't matter if you fail one day. Just get back up and try again the next day. This will be hard at first, but it will also become easier and easier as you travel along this path. Don't assume after failing for a week that 'I'm never going to get this' or 'these pillars are not right for me.' Just rise up, acknowledge and say, 'Ok, I broke my pillars today, but I will keep these going from now, and I will do my best.'

If you break it again tomorrow, then start the next day again. If you break it again, start the day after that. If you keep going and keep persisting, someday, one day, you will find freedom in living by these pillars, and the transformation inside your life will be a whole new experience for you.

People around you will notice a shift in your life. They will ask what has happened to you, they will comment on how your life is expanding, you will experience things you never thought possible, and you will wake up with the drive and determination to continue living by these five pillars,

1. Do Your Best

2. Use Your Word Wisely

3. Respect Others Model of The World

4. Assume Nothing

5. High Expectations, Detached Outcomes

### Pillar #1: Do Your Best

Remember that your best isn't always the highest you can do. The times you are fully alert and energised will produce higher results than when you are tired and exhausted. At the same time, you can still do your best in each situation. Your best will be better when you feel great as opposed to you feeling shitty or whether you are feeling cheerful and happy or pissed off, angry and jealous.

A strange thing happens when you start to do your best. You start to accept yourself for who you are, the mistakes you make, and the results you produce. You'll start to kill excuses and eradicate any sign of the bitch voice trying to talk you out of doing things. Doing your best leaves you with no regrets.

This 'do your best' mantra has been one of the biggest accelerators in my life. If you take one thing from this book, I urge you to try it out for 30 days and see what happens. I highly doubt that you will not want to continue living true to this Pillar.

## Pillar #2: Use Your Word Wisely

It is simple but very powerful. Since your thoughts and words represent your choices, learning how to think and speak to intentionally create what you desire can be of great value to your life.

Everything in your life is a projection of yourself. So whenever you use your word against someone else, and if they are your projection of you, you can see why it's hurting you. When you think about this to a deeper level, your projection of the world is how you want to see it. So when you change, your projection changes and the change you wish to see in the world will happen.

When you understand your words and what they can do, you'll begin to see many changes in your life. Changes first with how you deal with yourself and then how you deal with others.

When you can lock down this Pillar and master your words and thoughts, not only will you learn to not use your words against yourself, but others won't be able to use their words on you. They won't be able to get past your gatekeeper, and you'll just brush them off.

## Pillar #3: Respect Others Model of The World

Nothing others say or do directly results from you. It's a projection of their own reality, fantasy, and model of the world. Each and every one of us lives inside our reality in our 24-hour dreams or fantasy. Most men are already walking around asleep all the time, but it's not their fault; they just haven't been taught or shown how to become awake.

If you allow yourself to be affected by others' opinions, their judgements or even if they bother you in the slightest, they have your power. You are allowing them to use your power against you.

The path to personal freedom is not accepting others' opinions of you. If you receive a personal comment that hits you hard or provokes a reaction in you, that is something you must inquire about within yourself before accepting another's opinion. If someone says something that gets to me, all I ask is, why did that hurt me so much? What in that statement is triggering my insecurities? What is this person showing me that I need to work on within myself? This is a completely different way of looking at things and will lead to personal freedom.

## Pillar #4: Assume Nothing

We tend to make assumptions about everything. Because we are afraid to ask people to clarify in order to find out the truth, we enter into a cycle of assumptions. We are afraid to ask the hard questions we know we should be asking, fearing the answer we might not want to hear.

We only see what we want to see, hear what we want to hear, and believe what we want to believe. To end up only perceiving the bits we want to perceive and, on the whole, not seeing them the way they are. So as soon as you form an assumption or opinion, you'll start searching for 'evidence' to back that up.

To stop making these assumptions, you can do one simple thing: ASK! Ask questions if you don't understand or aren't 100% clear. Have the courage to ask questions, even if they are hard. Don't not ask a question because you are scared of the answer; this will lead to a hard and lacking life.

Action equals Change. When you take consistent action, you'll build new habits and strengthen your ability to do them unconsciously. This is where the magic happens. Un-desired unconscious to conscious to desired unconscious. Asleep to aware to awakened.

## Pillar #5: High Expectations, Detached Outcomes

If you speak to many life coaches, a lot of them will say that releasing your expectations will lead to happiness, but this is only one side of the equation. On one side, we'll never get anywhere; on the other, it can cause a lot of stress, worry and unhappiness.

When our reality doesn't match our expectations, we can become discouraged and begin to suffer. So many of us have our age attached as the timeframe we expect to have achieved certain milestones. If we fail to hit it by then, we feel the pain and unhappiness it causes.

In this new model, the expectations drive the outcome, not your happiness. Your happiness is determined by being content in your inner world, and you don't let these expectations determine your happiness.

Life is a lesson, and we learn best from our mistakes. If you look back and dwell on it, regret any decisions or focus on how you failed, you will be upset.

First, we must start by eliminating the belief that our life results from circumstances beyond our control. Reflecting and growing from these unmet expectations means you accept responsibility for your emotions, actions and life.

Healthy expectations are ones where you can detach from the outcome, and this is the new model I'm showing you here. Don't let your dreams and aspirations die because you fear your expectations will affect your happiness.

The most important part of all this is that you will finally find liberation and have personal freedom over yourself and your world.

## KEY POINTS

**POINT #1:** It doesn't matter if you fail one day. Just get back up and try again the next day.

**POINT #2:** If you keep going and keep persisting, someday, one day, you will find freedom in living by these pillars, and the transformation inside your life will be a whole new experience for you.

**POINT #3:** People around you will notice a shift in your life. They will ask what has happened to you, they will comment on how your life is expanding, you will experience things you never thought possible, and you will wake up with the drive and determination to continue living by these five pillars,

1. Do Your Best
2. Use Your Word Wisely
3. Respect Others Model of The World
4. Assume Nothing
5. High Expectations, Detached Outcomes

# 20

## PART III: THE OVERVIEW

### THE 4 LAWS

*"It is not the beauty of a building you should look at; its the construction of the foundation that will stand the test of time."*
### - David Allan Coe

Living by the MMC and the Daily 8, which you will experience later on in this book, is one thing. What we also live by is a set of laws. A set of non-negotiable laws that every man inside the brotherhood not only lives by but follows and takes into every aspect of his life.

These non-negotiables are things that you will begin to not negotiate on. The Code, The Pillars and The Laws have become non-negotiables in my life. I know I must live by these in order to be the man and be in the position of power that I am in right now inside the kingdom and legacy I'm forever building.

I'm not saying you must adopt these laws or live by the code. That's for you to decide. But I can tell you now that every man I've ever introduced this to and has decided to adopt it does live by these laws, and they have become the non-negotiables they live by. These laws should follow your values, principles, and beliefs and define what you are and are unwilling to accept from others and what you will and won't accept from yourself.

I want you to remember that if your current laws work and your current life works, you would most likely not be here reading this book. Read that again. If your laws and your life worked, you would not be here reading this book. You would be somewhere else, somewhere different, doing something different. At some level, these laws and rules you currently live by do not work, but you now have the opportunity to accept and experience a new set of laws from a superior place.

These laws make up the foundation on top of The 5 Pillars. Just like a building, it would be impossible to build a roof on a building first. The foundation must be the first thing, and it must be a strong solid structure. Previously we built the below-ground foundation with The Pillars; now, we build the above-ground foundation with The Laws.

## The Foundation

Not only is it your decision to accept the laws, but it's another thing to actually live by them. By openly affirming and sharing with the people that matter in your life, 'These are the laws I live by.' In doing this, people will know what is important to you, and you will be able to easily tell which of those people in your life are the ones that are going to support you. More importantly, which ones are not.

Getting clear on what is important to you, what is in line with your values, and what you believe in can make a massive shift in all areas of your life.

In the beginning, living by a new set of laws will come with a whole new set of challenges. The biggest one is self-resistance, just like when any type of change occurs. To live on your own terms, you will need to shake off your current social shackles, swim upstream and learn not to give a shit what anyone else thinks.

I had a long list of events in my past where I gave a shit about what people thought of me. I didn't want to upset anyone, I didn't want anyone to not like me, and I lost my ability to be assertive in the areas I needed to be. Afraid to question anyone else's opinion, always follow along with their views and live by their set of laws. These laws I'm going to share with you are not the be-all-end-all. They are a starting point that will make the most impact in your life while allowing for your own laws to be added that align with your values and beliefs.

If you accept everything you are told, you will be unknowingly and unintentionally manipulated. This acceptance has caused some of the world's greatest suffering. Therefore, I urge you to question the outer world and question your own thoughts, feelings, and beliefs. The lack of self-examination and self-analysis leads us to misinterpretation, mistaken impressions, and in particular, our ignorance about ourselves. Stay true to what matters most, and stay true to yourself. Have the guts to be your own man, and live it the way you wish.

### Break The Expectations

The last thing I want you to consider is that life doesn't have a fixed path with fixed laws that you must take. Life doesn't come with a guide on how to become a man or what your roles are as a man. I see too many men choose a path, especially a career path, that has been set by their parents or societal beliefs of what they should do. They think they must follow this path to make their parents, community, or anyone else happy.

I needed to break free from what I thought were the expectations of others. I needed to break free from the expectation that I needed to 'stick to the same career,' break free from the current societal expectations of men, and break free from the 'hate' men have received lately. When you can break free from this, you don't even notice it.

I constantly see comments of guys writing about how attacked we are as men. How women are getting what they want when they want. How men are being grouped as toxic, and our masculinity is getting sucked out of us. Here's the thing, you can't have one without the other. So there are always two sides to the same coin. When you can live by The MMC and continue to do the inner work, you don't even notice it. All of the things I mentioned above, I don't notice anymore. They just don't bother me. I'm 100% happy and comfortable within myself that nothing external like that affects me. That's what I'm here for, to help you reach this place and for you to come join the club.

Now, let's move on as we review these laws and lay the upper ground foundation for how we can live these Laws as a reality.

## KEY POINTS

**POINT #1:** These laws make up the foundation on top of The 5 Pillars.

**POINT #2:** If your laws and your life worked, you would not be here reading this book. You would be somewhere else, somewhere different, doing something different.

**POINT #3:** Getting clear on what is important to you, what is in line with your values, and what you believe in can make a massive shift in all areas of your life.

**POINT #4:** When you can live by The MMC and continue to do the inner work, things just don't bother you. You'll become 100% happy and comfortable within yourself that nothing external will affects you.

# 21

# LAW NUMBER I

## BE PRESENT

*"Yesterday's the past, tomorrow's the future, but today is a gift. That's why it's called the present."*
## - Bil Keane

In the stressful and chaotic days we face as we go about our daily lives, we tend to shift our focus to everywhere but right here, in the present. How do we deal with this, and where do we need to shift that focus? The answer is simple: Be Present. Being present and focused will produce the results that you are after.

If you constantly live in the future, you maybe start to worry or be anxious about 'what the future holds'. AKA anxiety. If you live in the past, you probably have a lot of regret, guilt, shame and fears. It's not uncommon for people living in the past to be dealing with addictions, taking drugs and drinking too much.

These forms of 'escape' do one thing. They allow you to forget what's happening in your life and bring you to what is happening in the now. When you are living in the now, you are present. So alcohol and drugs bring you back to becoming more present. This is why so many of my clients come to me with drinking or drug problems, and I say to them that it will naturally clear over time as we work on some other underlying things. When you are present, you don't need to escape. When you are happy within yourself, you don't need to escape.

## Being Present Can Be Your Shelter

No matter how chaotic your day is, no matter how stressful your job or life becomes, the act of being present can become your shelter. It can change your life, and it's incredibly simple. Simple, yes. But easy? No.

Right now, learn to focus completely on doing the thing that you are doing and nothing else. Become aware of what you are doing and every aspect involved inside your body and your thoughts. Your thoughts will naturally jump around, and that's fine, but the art of being present is to bring yourself back to the present task at hand as soon as you notice your mind drifting off. This is why meditation is so important.

It will be no surprise to hear that many men can't multitask. Multitasking is really just switching from one thing to another in quick succession or mixing similar tasks with ones that are automatic. Like walking, for example. This is why having the ability to maintain focus on just the one task at hand and do it wholeheartedly and with 100% effort is so important. In fact, no one can multitask things that take mental capacity. As much as we might think we are multitasking, all we are doing is rapidly shifting our focus between the two tasks, so it seems that we are multitasking when in reality, our focus is just going back and forth between tasks.

## Present Communication

As I mentioned earlier in this book, I struggled a lot in social situations throughout my teens and early 20s. I always felt uneasy, constantly worried about saying the wrong thing and never actually enjoyed being in social situations. I wanted to meet new people, but it was hard for me. As I reflect on those situations, I realise I was everywhere but there. My mind was creating situations and worrying instead of being present. No wonder why I never knew what to say; I never really listened to what they were saying as I was too caught up in my head.

When you are present and focused, you'll never not know what to say. You'll be so involved in the conversation that the words will just flow. This is exactly the same for me when I first started speaking at events. As soon as I shifted to thinking about what I would say next, or if I started to worry about what others were doing or thinking, I lost my train of thought and my words. Again, because I was too caught up in my head.

The number of people I see that are not present. People go to dinner and sit on their phones. People are distracted by things they should do next. They worry about having so much to do. If you keep living that way, your life in this physical body will be over before you know it. Enjoy the moments you have on this earth; the best way to do that is to be present.

If you can be present around your partner and kids and give them your undivided attention, you will have a great relationship with them all. I'm not talking about just being physically present; I'm talking about being energetically present as well. Send your energy to them and let them feel your presence. People crave to be wanted by others, and you doing this is sending that message that you want and care for them. What you put out, you get back in return, so it will come back to you.

## Missing The Moment

Most of our time is spent in the past or the future rather than being in the present moment. We are letting the present moment pass us by and moving on to the next one. In doing so, we miss the moment. We may be so focused on reaching that new goal, chasing that dream or whatever it may be, that we forget to stop and take it all in. Don't get me wrong, those are great things, and you should be going after new goals and targets, but don't forget to stop and enjoy the present moment. I spent years of my life as a FIFO worker wishing my life away. I was focused on making it to the next time I could come home and disregarded everything in between. I was miserable, and I'm sure I would have been a boring person to be around back then.

Take your time to enjoy the same things in life and be present as often as possible. If you don't, life will end up just passing you by, and the truth is that we are doing this to ourselves. Life only ever has and will only ever exist in the present: it's only ever now. It's never yesterday, and it's never tomorrow. It's not even ever later today. Moments create our experiences, and the experiences are what we remember. Experiences are only ever created in the present.

So, live by law number I: Be Present as often as possible. I don't want you to look back at your life 10-20-30 years from now and realise how much you've missed out on. Time is really the only thing we have, so make the most of it on this amazing planet we live on.

## KEY POINTS

**POINT #1:** Being present and focused will produce the results that you are after.

**POINT #2:** If you constantly live in the future, you maybe start to worry or be anxious about 'what the future holds'. AKA anxiety.

**POINT #3:** If you live in the past, you probably have a lot of regret, guilt, shame and fears. It's not uncommon for people living in the past to be dealing with addictions, taking drugs and drinking too much.

**POINT #4:** When you are present, you don't need to escape. When you are happy within yourself, you don't need to escape.

**POINT #5:** Enjoy the moments you have on this earth; the best way to do that is to be present.

**POINT #6:** Take your time to enjoy the simple things in life and be present as often as possible. If you don't, life will end up just passing you by, and the truth is that we are doing this to ourselves.

**POINT #7:** Time is really the only thing we have, so make the most of it on this amazing planet we live on.

# 22

## LAW NUMBER II

### FACTS & DETAILS COUNT

*"I went to the woods because I wished
to live deliberately, to front only the
essential facts of life, and see if I could
not learn what it had to teach, and not,
when I came to die, discover that I had
not lived."*
**- Henry David Thoreau**

What goes into your life and the experiences you create matters to you, your family, and your friends. How you choose to spend your time ultimately determines where your priorities lie. We put most of our attention and time into the things that matter to us most and those that fulfil our highest values.

We live in a society that is always on the go. We have become used to neglecting the finer details in life, imagining that they don't and won't count for much. I am able to look back on my life and recognise which facts were the ones that helped in my success and which led to short-term failure. It all comes down to the facts.

How far you are willing to dive into the facts will determine what you will learn. Most of our 'failures' in life don't come from the big things falling down. It comes from the small things slowly crumbling down below: the small things that so often get pushed to the side, the small things that get ignored, the small things that you shy away from, and the small things that you pretend are not there. These are what we think don't matter all that much until we realise they are just as important.

### Stop Lying & Pretending

If you are unwilling to look at the facts, you will stay stuck in your current situation. The longer you stay stuck here, the hard it will become to get yourself out of this hole you've dug for yourself. We all know sticking your head in the sand will not make any problems disappear, so why does it still happen! Pretending everything is 'good' or 'ok' when it's not will lead you down a hard road later in life. Maybe even a mid-life crisis will be on the cards.

For most men, it's easier for us to pretend like our life is good and we don't see any problems. We have become so content with avoiding the facts of our lives and always taking the easy road. Deep down, we know something is going on, but we're not willing at the time to address it. When you address the facts of your life, the pretending will stop.

The number of men who come to me who are going through relation-ship problems is outstanding and quite disappointing, to be honest. Most of them seem to all say; I thought things were going well until she just left one day, called the police on them, told them she was cheating or whatever other method she'd used to get rid of him. I'm not saying it's always the case with relationship break-ups, but it's way more common than not.

After a few sessions and we get down to a few deep-rooted causes of their issue, it always comes out that these same men who first told me they 'got blindsided' by their relationship breakdown could now see it was coming. If they didn't pretend things were good and paid attention to the facts, half of them wouldn't be in the position they are right now. Stop lying to yourself, stop pretending your life is 'good' and face the facts. Yes, it might be hard or confronting at first, but it will be worth it.

### Peel Back The Band-Aid

Let's say you are willing to peel back the band-aid of your life and get to facts; where do you start? First, be prepared to get real, raw and honest with yourself. I do this once a year and expose the underlying weakness that I may not be willing to see or accept. Start with your Body. Take your shirt off. Are you happy with the man you are looking at in the mirror? Are you happy with how you look? How are your eating habits? How is your relationship with alcohol or drugs? How often do you work out? Those are the facts.

Then move on to your Mind. How are your stress levels, or how do you manage them? How often do you meditate? How is your spiritual connection with the Universe/God/Spirit/Source? How is your relationship with yourself? How many times have you completed a Flip? Those are facts.

Next, we move on to Bond – connection and relationships. How is your relationship with your partner? Do you even have a partner? What are the things that aren't working in your relationship? How often do you have sex? How close do you feel to your friends and family? How is your relationship with your kids? Do they enjoy spending time with you, or are you nonexistent? Those are facts.

Finally, Money. How are your spending habits? How well do you track your money? Where are you at financially right now? How driven or motivated do you feel in your career? Do you even have a career? What skills do you need to improve? Are you happy with your career? Those are the facts.

## Win With The Details

As you start to progress and achieve success in any area of life, it's easy to get caught up in all this and forget the smaller details. You forget that these finer details were the ones that led you to get to where you are now. As you experience change and start to improve your life, your vision and goals start to get bigger. You begin to think bigger, take bigger actions and look for bigger tasks.

What happens when we begin to have bigger success is that we forget where that success started. It was from doing the small, consistent actions regularly. This seems to get thrown out the window. We stop paying attention to the details. They seem so small that if we were to let it slide for a day or two, it doesn't make a noticeable difference.

Before you know it, one day becomes a week. One week becomes one month. One month becomes one year. Then suddenly, it seems like from nowhere, it all comes tumbling down. It leaves you sitting there asking yourself, 'where the fuck did I go wrong?'

When you don't pay attention to these finer details and don't see how important they are, it will be exactly the facts of your undoing. This can be a huge price to pay if you do this in all areas of life.

Think about this, if you don't pay attention to the smaller details of your heath. You skip a few workouts, you slack off on your eating habits, you start drinking a little more, and you never go for a checkup or get your bloodwork done. Thinking it may not be all that big of a deal, until one day you look back at a photo and realise you've got really fat. Maybe you get a sudden call from the doctor informing you that you have a heart condition.

If you don't pay attention to the details inside your relationship, you stop doing little things for each other, you stop putting as much effort in, you stop communicating as often, or you stop taking her for date night. You will end up in a separation before you know it.

If you don't keep track of your finances, of what's coming in and out, you'll begin to spend more, you'll be stressing about what you can and can't afford, and you'll end up in an even worse financial position.

From now on, I want you to acknowledge the importance of details. They can be the difference between a failure and a success, an opportunity and a missed opportunity, maybe even life and death.

We tend to move through our lives without realising that the Universe/God/Spirit/Source, whatever you believe in, has provided us with everything we require to live an abundant life full of fulfilment. Sometimes it can be hard for us to see the bigger picture for you and your life. This is where you must have faith. Faith in the knowledge that the details and facts count and that adding these smaller details together will slowly add up to create the big picture. This is why law number II is: Facts Count.

## KEY POINTS

**POINT #1:** We put most of our attention and time into the things that matter to us most and those that fulfil our highest values.

**POINT #2:** How far you are willing to dive into the facts will determine what you will learn.

**POINT #3:** If you are unwilling to look at the facts, you will stay stuck in your current situation.

**POINT #4:** The longer you stay stuck here, the hard it will become to get yourself out of this hole you've dug for yourself.

**POINT #5:** We begin to have bigger success is that we forget where that success started; we stop paying attention to the details.

**POINT #6:** They can be the difference between a failure and a success, an opportunity and a missed opportunity, maybe even life and death.

# 23

## LAW NUMBER III

### DON'T EVER GIVE UP

*"Our greatest weakness lies in giving up. The most certain way to succeed is always to try just one more time."*
**- Thomas A. Edison**

I have no doubt that life can be hard at times, and it's certainly not always fair. Sometimes it hurts, and it kicks you when you're down. In times like these, you'll come to realise what power you have within to change yourself for the better. You will have something inside of you that is stronger than whatever that thing is that is holding you down. You can, and you will find it, and you will be stronger because of it. Life only throws you challenges and problems that you can handle. If you get dealt a challenge like this, it means you are up for it.

If we go back to law number II, some of the smaller details in your life may be hard. They may seem like an obstacle holding you back, but they'll lead you to a higher place if you do not ever give up. I would go as far as saying there are millions of men in Australia and hundreds of millions worldwide that could be living much better lives, filled with confidence, happiness, fulfilment and success, but they aren't. They could be achieving so many amazing things and living to their true potential, but they aren't. They could change their lives and be a positive role model for their children, but they aren't.

Why? Because they listen to that little voice in the back of their head that says things are too hard, they can't do this, or they can't do that, and they quit. Leaving so much potential and gifts inside themselves and taking them to their graves. When you commit to never giving up, you will succeed eventually. It may talk ten times longer than expected, but you will make it there. If you quit and give up, you'll never get there.

Becoming your greatest version, a king, building a kingdom and leaving your legacy is not easy; it has never been and never will be. If it were easy, then every man would have done it. If easy is what you want, plenty of 'easy' is out there. Drugs, alcohol, sex, porn, masturbation, gaming, Netflix, you name it. Here at AMD and inside this brotherhood, we don't do whatever is easy; we do whatever is needed and never give up on it.

### Do Hard Things & Your Life Will Be Easy

This was a concept I took to the extreme, and I still do. I recently completed 75HARD, but halfway through, I decided it was too easy, so I went 100 days. Why? Because I know my life will get easier if I do hard things now. But it's not actually that life gets easier; it's just that you become better so those smaller challenges don't phase you.

When you commit to never giving up, you are building mental toughness and sending a powerful signal to your unconscious mind that you will complete anything you put your mind to. Being mentally strong in a world with so many mentally weak and struggling people will give you an unfair advantage in life. Not that this is a game of who is better or anything like that. It's simply about being the best you can be. When you are at your best and are mentally tough, you are in a position where you can help others and lift them up.

I would not be able to help change the lives of 100s of men if I hadn't first put in the work and built mental strength. Helping men wasn't even my plan until I reached this place. Maybe that's what your journey may lead to as well. There are so many other coaches, therapists, professionals, and gurus who haven't built this themselves and are now trying to help others. Maybe it's their passion, which is cool, but the work needs to be done first. Overweight personal trainers, psychologists who drink every night, and doctors who are not healthy, are perfect examples of this.[29] They are examples that they: 1. Haven't committed to doing hard things, and 2. They have given up on themselves in some areas. No hate, just facts.

### You Will Only Ever Fail If You Quit

When your back is against the wall, the last thing you can do is quit. I can say without hesitation; that you will want to give up. You will want to throw in the towel. I have plenty of times before, and in one of my darkest places, when the voice inside said to me, 'are you really going to give up that easy?'. I made the decision to step down and not quit on life. That is where the tagline 'you're only one decision away...' and the law 'don't ever give up' came from and why I hold them so close.

When I say 'don't ever give up,' I'm not only referring to giving up on life. I'm talking about giving up on everything. If you give up, you lose. You let yourself down, and you let down the others around you. So what happens when you get to this place where you want to give up? What do you do when you have had enough? You aren't alone on this journey. Although you may be reading, watching, and learning on your own, know that there is a brotherhood of men just like you and me striving for that same desire in life.

This is not a competition, nor is it a race, and there is enough room for us all to have the lives we want to build. When times get tough, and you feel like giving up, reach out to any of the brothers inside AMD and immerse yourself in this one-of-a-kind support system. This isn't a place for perfect men with perfect lives. This is a place for men like you to be met where you are currently standing and grow along with you on your journey to becoming the man you desire to become.

Law number I: Be Present, Law number II: Facts & Details Count, Law number III: Don't Ever Give Up, and Law number IV: TTP.

## KEY POINTS

**POINT #1:** Life can be hard at times, and it's certainly not always fair. Sometimes it hurts, and it kicks you when you're down. In times like these, you'll come to realise what power you have within to change yourself for the better.

**POINT #2:** Life will get easier if you do hard things now. But it's not actually that life gets easier; it's just that you become better so those smaller challenges don't phase you.

**POINT #3:** When you commit to never giving up, you are building mental toughness and sending a powerful signal to your unconscious mind that you will complete anything you put your mind to.

**POINT #4:** Being mentally strong in a world with so many mentally weak and struggling people will give you an unfair advantage in life.

**POINT #5:** You aren't alone on this journey. We are here with you at every step.

# 24

## LAW NUMBER IV

### TTP – TRUST THE PROCESS

*"No man is free who is not master of himself."*
**- Epictetus**

This fourth and final law again is simple: trust the process and do the work. There is no longer a possibility that this 'might' work or a question 'if' it works. I say with the certainty of 'when' it works, and it 'will' work. This system within the MMC has changed my life, it's changed the lives of men inside the brotherhood who have personally worked with me, and it will do the same for you if you commit, trust the process, and do the work.

Trusting the process can be hard for a lot of men. Instant gratification is the driving force that stops us from fully trusting the process. We want stuff now and for it to happen right now. If there are no results within a week, scrap that idea, and it's onto the next. Constantly chasing the new red shiny object with the new secret magic pill to solve your problems. The fitness industry is prevalent for this: the new diet, the new workout plan, the new supplement. What really works is consistency and commitment.

The term overnight success is widely used for someone who has achieved something in his life that others think came out of nowhere. What people aren't willing to see is the hours and hours of work they've done in the background in the years leading up to this. These are the facts; unfortunately, some don't want to see them. I can tell you that no one has reached success, and we're talking about success in any area of life without trusting the process.

By trusting in the process, you're allowing what IS to be what it IS. It means continuing down that path many times, regardless of the results. It means letting go of control and expectations. It means taking the most effective action in a relaxed state at any moment. Trust is knowing that no matter what happens, it's all part of life's journey.

### Trusting Doesn't Mean The Process Is Easy

When you let go of trying to control every aspect and attempting to control the end result, you'll gain a much more fulfilling experience by just allowing life to happen. Letting go of control can be the hardest part for men, especially if your career calls for you to be in control. It's a masculine trait to be in control. When you feel any negative attitudes, statements, or behaviours disrupting the process, you must do what you can to limit them.

Trusting the process allows life to be what it is without steering, manipulating, or controlling your behaviours or actions to deviate off course, thinking it will get you what you want faster. It requires you to build discipline and perseverance to keep going when it feels like you aren't getting anywhere.

Early 2022, I was in a private group session with Regan Hillyer,[30] the manifesting queen. Yes, it's a little woo-woo but stay with me here. Something amazing happened during this session, and it perfectly fitted this law of trusting the process. Towards the end of the session, we were asked to bring up two mental mirrors, one with the current version of ourselves and one with the future version which had achieved the goal we wanted to achieve.

I asked this future version for a piece of advice that was going to allow me to achieve what I wanted. Guess what he said? Follow the process, and it will work out. I smiled. Talk about listening to your own advice! After this happened, still with my eyes closed, I flew out into the future to the date I wanted to achieve this. I saw it there, sitting in my future at about 4 months away. As I flew back to the present, looking over any challenges, I kept experiencing the same thing, just trust the process. At every challenge, it was just a matter of trusting the process. The best part about this is that instead of it happening in four months, I achieved it in two.

The point I want to make is that it was easy for me to see how trusting the process was the only thing I needed to focus on. The rest just all fell into place. The same will be true with you. I have given you the plan, the foundation, the framework and the code, now it's up to you to just trust the process, and it will work for you. Hopefully, in half the time you may have planned.

## When You Do The Work, The Work Works

I can't do the work for you, nor will I or anybody else do it for you. By me or somebody else doing it for you, we would be doing the work, not you. Therefore, you will not reach the place you want to go. A king never became a king by sitting back and letting others do shit for him. A king is a king because he has done the work and trusts the process along with the work he has done.

What do I mean when I say do the work? Doing the work is simple: living by The Laws, The Pillars, and The Code, weaponising yourself with the Daily 8, hitting the targets and benchmarks, consistently completing The Flips inside the King's Journal, and staying real, raw, honest, and true to yourself and everyone else inside your world.

There is no guarantee that working hard will get you where you want to be, but you can't get to where you want to be without it. So hard work is necessary. Hey, if you don't want to do the work, maybe this isn't for you. If you are prepared to put in the work and effort, you will be rewarded 10 fold. Many people work hard or think they are working hard, but they don't really have a plan of what they are doing. It's kind of like digging a hole just for the sake of being busy and working hard.

The difference is you have everything laid out for you here. It's now up to you to execute and put in the work. Once you do that, the only thing left is to trust the process. That is the final part of doing the work, trusting in the process that the work you have done and are doing will work.

## KEY POINTS

**POINT #1:** This system within the MMC has changed the lives of men inside the brotherhood, and it will do the same for you if you commit, trust the process, and do the work.

**POINT #2:** Instant gratification is the driving force that stops us from fully trusting the process. We want stuff now and for it to happen right now.

**POINT #3:** When you let go of trying to control every aspect and attempting to control the end result, you'll gain a much more fulfilling experience by just allowing life to happen.

**POINT #4:** It's now up to you to execute and put in the work. Once you do that, the only thing left is to trust the process.

# 25

# PART III: THE SUMMARY

## THE 4 LAWS

*"We are what our thoughts have made us; so take care about what you think. Words are secondary. Thoughts live; they travel far."*
## - Swami Vivekananda

The final piece before we move on to the last part of this book is being able to live by the four laws. A set of non-negotiable laws that every man inside the brotherhood not only lives by but follows and takes into every aspect of his life.

I can't tell you how to live your life or what laws you should follow; that's ultimately your decision. But if you want to experience the transformational process of living by the MMC, the laws will become non-negotiable for you over time.

I want you to consider that you would not be here if your current laws and your life were working. Now that you are here, I also want you to consider the impact of adopting these four laws will have on your life.

## Law I: Be Present

If you constantly live in the future, you maybe start to worry or be anxious about 'what the future holds'. AKA anxiety. If you live in the past, you probably have a lot of regret, guilt, shame and fears. When you are present, none of this can exist.

No matter how chaotic your day is, no matter how stressful your job or life becomes, the act of being present can become your shelter. It can change your life, and it's incredibly simple. Learn to focus completely on doing the thing that you are doing and nothing else. Become aware of what you are doing and every aspect involved inside your body and your thoughts.

Most of our time is spent in the past or the future rather than being in the present moment. We are letting the present moment pass us by and moving on to the next one. In doing so, we miss the moment.

Take your time to enjoy the same things in life and be present as often as possible. If you don't, life will end up just passing you by, and the truth is that we are doing this to ourselves.

## Law II: Facts & Details Count

How far you are willing to dive into the facts will determine what you will learn. Most of our 'failures' in life don't come from the big things falling down, but from the small things slowly crumbling down below.

If you are unwilling to look at the facts, you will stay stuck in your current situation. The longer you stay stuck here, the hard it will become to get yourself out of this hole you've dug for yourself. Sticking your head in the sand will not make any problems disappear.

When you don't pay attention to these finer details and don't see how important they are, it will be exactly the facts of your undoing. This can be a huge price to pay if you do this in all areas of life. They can be the difference between a failure and a success, an opportunity and a missed opportunity, maybe even life and death.

## Law III: Don't Ever Give Up

That little voice in the back of your head that says things are too hard, you can't do this, or you can't do that, will cause you to quit. Many men leave so much potential and gifts inside themselves and take them to their graves. When you commit to never giving up, you will succeed eventually. It may talk ten times longer than expected, but you will make it there. If you quit and give up, you'll never get there.

Becoming your greatest version, a king, building a kingdom and leaving your legacy is not easy; it has never been and never will be. If it were easy, then every man would have done it. If easy is what you want, plenty of 'easy' is out there.

Here at AMD and inside this brotherhood, we don't do whatever is easy; we do whatever is needed and never give up on it.

When you commit to never giving up, you are building mental toughness and sending a powerful signal to your unconscious mind that you will complete anything you put your mind to. Being mentally strong in a world with so many mentally weak and struggling people will give you an unfair advantage in life.

If you give up, you lose. You let yourself down, and you let down the others around you.

## Law IV: TTP

There is no longer a possibility that this 'might' work or a question of 'if' it works. I say with the certainty of 'when' it works, and it 'will' work. This system within the MMC has changed my life, it's changed the lives of men inside the brotherhood who have personally worked with me, and it will do the same for you if you commit, trust the process, and do the work.

When you let go of trying to control every aspect and attempting to control the end result, you'll gain a much more fulfilling experience by just allowing life to happen. Letting go of control can be the hardest part for men, especially if your career calls for you to be in control.

I can't do the work for you, nor will I or anybody else do it for you. By me or somebody else doing it for you, we would be doing the work, not you. Therefore, you will not reach the place you want to go. A king is a king because he has done the work and trusts the process along with the work he has done.

The difference is you have everything laid out for you here. It's now up to you to execute and put in the work. Once you do that, the only thing left is to trust the process. When you want to give in and quit, come back to these 4 Laws.

From here, we move on to the final part of the MMC, the Daily 8. Well done on getting this far. Part IV will be what amplifies your results at an accelerated pace.

## KEY POINTS

**POINT #1:** If you want to experience the transformational process of living by the MMC, the laws will become non-negotiable for you over time.

**POINT #2:** You have everything laid out for you here.

**POINT #3:** It's now up to you to execute and put in the work. Once you do that, the only thing left is to trust the process.

**POINT #4:** When you want to give in and quit, come back to these 4 Laws.

1. Law I: Be Present
2. Law II: Facts & Details Count
3. Law III: Don't Ever Give Up
4. Law IV: TTP

# 26

# PART IV: THE OVERVIEW

## THE DAILY 8

*"Power is of two kinds. One is obtained by the fear of punishment and the other by acts of love. Power based on love is a thousand times more effective and permanent then the one derived from fear of punishment."*
- **Mahatma Gandhi**

The Daily 8. What is it? And what does it entail? It's the eight daily habits that allow The Foundation – Part I, II, and III – to be now used as we build on top of it. It becomes the next step in providing a very real and practical set of tasks that will expand your capacity to do more and be more as fast as possible.

Your ability to complete every one of the Daily 8 equips you with power that will allow you to win that day. Winning just one day doesn't seem like much, but when the effect is added up from winning each and every day, the cumulative results are unbelievable. Your friends, family, and loved ones will start to notice, and they will start to wonder about the work you have been doing.

### Started from A Damaged Man

It wasn't as if one day I woke up and decided that today I would stack my morning with most of the Daily 8 elements. I didn't even know at the time it would even develop into what is now known as the Daily 8. It came because my world was broken, and I was a damaged man. My life wasn't working, and I had no idea how to fix it.

What I did know is that my life went in phases. My body would be in good shape, but my mind, relationships, and social life would suck. There would also be phases where I would be making and saving money, but my mind was not happy. Then there would be times when I would have great relationships, but my body would suffer, and I would burn through cash. Come to think of it now, I'd say my mind was never in good shape compared to what it is now.

I just couldn't find that place where I had all four dimensions running in alignment with each other: Body, Mind, Bond, Money. I'd have one or two working, but the others would be either suffering or non-existent.

### When the Tide Goes Out

For most people, when the tide goes out, the rocks are exposed, and so is the reality of their life. I say most people because the opposite was the case for me. The tide was up with my money and the financial position I was in, but it exposed some harsh realities about myself that were nearly all too much for me to handle at the time. My body was weak from the constant crash-dieting, my social life was shattered, and

I had no desire to interact with anyone. At this time, my mind led me down some dark roads. Just after this and amidst my internal chaos, I was actually learning the truth in my life about what was working for me and what was not.

One day, I realised that when my workouts and nutrition were aligned, I had more energy, tended to be just a little bit happier, and enjoyed life a little more. I had always been competing in some type of sport from a young age, so this experience wasn't all that new to me. And this game made sense to me due to the endorphins released after exercise.

What didn't make sense was how I could keep these two elements running in alignment while also bringing up my social life and relationships, my production level, and my ability to make money to reach that same level.

I was sitting at a conference when the next speaker called up on stage was someone I'd never heard of. He went on to introduce himself and how great his life was. He had an immaculate palace he called home with his beautiful wife and two baby girls. His presentation also showed his private home gym while he was working out. I couldn't comprehend the idea that he seemed to 'have it all' in Body, Mind, Bond, and Money.

### Backed by Results

After watching this man speak during that conference, his results in life really intrigued me. 'How is it possible that this guy can have such a perfect life?' That man went by the name of David Leon.[31]

This led me down the path of constantly striving for alignment in all four dimensions of my life, using David as a role model. I'm sure he wouldn't have any idea of the impact he's had on my life. Still, I'm always grateful for being at the conference that day, which ultimately led to the discovery of the Daily 8.

If I wanted results in my body, I would add a daily task that got me that result; if I wanted results in my relationships, I would add another daily task that guided me towards those results. It was the same in all four areas.

I've spend years adding and testing new tasks while removing the ones that weren't giving me as much an impact. As a result of constent refinement, the Daily 8 has been developed into my non-negotiable routine for the day. If I do not get in all 8, I feel off, and I don't get as much done as I know I can. The daily 8 keeps me running at a pace that seems impossible for other men to achieve.

## The Impossible Speed

Others constantly ask me, 'How do you get so much done? How do you always have energy? How do you always look like you are having fun? How do you maintain the body you have?'

My answer is always, 'From completing my Daily 8 religiously.' These tasks help me and every other man inside this brotherhood to continue to make the impossible possible with the speed they run at. Each of the Daily 8 has its dedicated chapter that details how they came about and the profound effects they will have on your life.

## Task to Habit = Power

Right now, I don't think about completing my Daily 8; they just happen like habits. When I say just happen, it doesn't mean I just cruise through them. I work even harder than the day before, but my body knows exactly what is the next task. I habit stack my morning as it allows my power and production to excel not only from the work within the Daily 8 but also by the space it creates in my head by not needing to think about what I need to do.

Habit stacking is a term and idea I got from a book called *Atomic Habits* by the author James Clear.[32] The whole concept of creating a new habit is as simple as attaching it to a habit you already do. Getting out of bed is a habit; making your bed is a habit, and brushing your teeth in the morning is a habit. This is how you can turn a task into a habit.

Once one of these new tasks becomes a habit, the next task can be attached, again, making it a habit. This is habit stacking, and I stack 5 of the Daily 8 on top of each other every single morning. Whether I'm travelling, had a late night, or it's a weekend. The Daily 8 has become a series of habits that I look forward to completing and are never a hassle. When you reach this place, you are in a place of extreme power.

## KEY POINTS

**POINT #1:** The Daily 8 provides a real and practical set of tasks that will expand your capacity to do more and be more as fast as possible.

**POINT #2:** Your ability to complete every one of the Daily 8 equips you with power that will allow you to win that day.

**POINT #3:** Winning just one day doesn't seem like much, but when the effect is added up from winning each and every day, the cumulative results are unbelievable.

**POINT #4:** Each of the Daily 8 has its dedicated chapter that details how they came about and the profound effects they will have on your life.

**POINT #5:** When the Daily 8 has become a series of habits you look forward to completing and are never a hassle, you are in a place of extreme power.

# 27

# THE DAILY 8: #1

## WORKOUT

*"Just do some kind of workout. Doesn't matter if it's going for a walk around the block, going for a jog, doing some calisthenics, lifting weights, going to a pool and swimming - you name it. But do something that gets your blood flowing and gets your mind in the game."*
## - Jocko Willink

The body you are standing in is the only one you will ever get. Think about that for a second. This body, YOUR body, is the only one you will ever get. It will never be like a car or a phone where after a few years of work it starts to break down and fall apart. We just replace it with a new and the latest model and don't think twice about it. Although our body can definitely feel like a car or phone at times, feeling flat and out of fuel, it certainly cannot be replaced after a few years of work.

There are no latest model upgrades or replacements for your body. I don't care about the latest and greatest improvements in regenerative medicine. A replacement will never work as well as the original. Plus, it's still a while before anything like that becomes widespread and affordable for the masses.

Some men forget about this. They get complacent with the fact that they will wake up every morning the same way as they did the last. Taking every day as it comes with no thought of what they are doing or not doing in the way of health and fitness. Unfortunately, it generally takes something bad to happen to our bodies for us to wake up to the fact that we have been neglecting them. You feel surprised when the doctor says that you have a heart problem or diabetes, or you jump on the scales to see you've gained 10kg. This is no surprise! It's the result of a lack of awareness and care for yourself.

I remember coming home from a three-month trip around Europe in my early 20s. I came home like a little fatty. One of the first things my mother mentioned was the extra fat around my face and neck. It was the first thing she noticed about me. I spent the next few months complaining about how fat I was and how I just wanted to be back to the shape I was previously in. Here's the truth: deep down, I knew what I was doing while travelling, and I knew that I was gaining some serious fat. But I chose to ignore it and pretend it wasn't that bad. I was willingly abusing and neglecting my body with the excuse that, 'I'm just enjoying myself.'

Until I got back to my previous weight, I felt like shit every day I woke up. My energy was used up by 10 am, my drive was virtually gone, and any suggestion of working sounded like a big effort. I needed to throw down excessive amounts of pre-workout just to get to the gym. The simple fact is I still went, and I got back to my previous weight.

You may be wondering why this has anything to do with you becoming the best man you can be.

Well, it's simple. You cannot build and lead as a man if you get out of breath from walking up two sets of stairs. You cannot have passionate sex if you only get in 30 seconds before you need a break. You cannot desire to build anything great if all you want to do is sit on the couch, eat pizza, drink beer, and watch TV.

### The Facts

Let's look at the facts. Think about the last week and how many times you have worked out? How many times have you worked out in the last month? Do you give a shit about your body, and what does your body have to show whether you do or not? How does the state of your body represent the way you treat it?

Look at your body in the mirror, your butt-naked body; what does it have to say about you? Are you impressed? Do you think it's attractive to your partner? What message are you sending to your kids or future kids? This might sound harsh, and it might bring up some emotional sore spots for you, but here's the thing. You are here, and if you decide to live and follow this Code, you are going to see improvements. We all have to start somewhere. To start, you need to be clear where you are starting from, rather than hiding behind clothes or bullshit stories that justify the way your body is right now. Get real, raw, and honest about why you are here and give yourself the permission you need to STOP hiding behind these lies.

Men worldwide run their bodies at 50 or 60% total capacity, and they expect great things to happen. If anything else inside your life was running at the same 50-60% capacity, what do you think would happen to that, and how long would it last?

What if your job or business only paid you 50% because you only put in 50% effort? What if you were only 50% committed to your partner, and she was 50% towards you? See what I mean?

## Decide

You have got to decide how you will view your body. Will it give you access to the abundance of power and energy you could have available, or is it going to be a barrier between who you are now and the Superior You? Depending on where you are right now, do you consider your body to be a weapon, or could you see it becoming a weapon you use to produce the results you deserve and desire?

Playing sport has been a big part of my life after I was pushed into it by my parents at an early age. I've always loved to compete and couldn't imagine my life without fitness, but the definition of training is completely different for me now. Throughout my teenage years, it was always a game of determining the least amount of effort I could put in just to get through the session.

During my final year in high school and in the middle of pre-season of what would be my biggest rugby season to date, there'd be a full squad fitness session every Friday morning before school. One of the go-to drills used by our coaches was the full field sprint. 17 seconds were all we needed to complete each sprint. What do you think was the average time it took us? Probably around 16.5 seconds.

I can't tell you how often I walk around the gym only to see someone sitting on their phone or being a social butterfly for 45 minutes, leaving soon after because they needed to run. I can't tell you how often I've seen men plan to start a new fitness routine only to fall off two weeks later. I can't tell you how often I see men only doing what they 'have to' regarding their fitness.

This is not about turning you into an athlete, nor is it about turning you into a gym junkie or CrossFit groupie. Unless you want to, of course. The principle is simple, your body and your fitness level are the gateways to your power and energy. They are directly responsible for the way you look and feel. Your *lack* of power and energy is a direct response to the fitness that you don't have.

Years of abuse, neglect and addictions beat down the body you live in, day by day, month by month, year by year. Severely reducing your running capacity invites viruses and cancers to join in on the deconstruction.

## Be The Master, Not The Servant

When you wake up in the morning, do you rise feeling like a god or a hostage? Most men roll out of bed and end up being hostage to their bodies. They are becoming slaves to the body's cravings and addictions. The body is the master instead of being the servant. The body dictates how you act, what you do, and where you go.

I had to deal with several addictions of my own. What I did to suppress the feelings and emotions I was experiencing inside my head caused chaos inside my body. From working out and training ridiculous amounts at ridiculous intensities: sometimes 3-4 sessions a day, 5-6 hrs a single day. I was masking the reality that I was too scared to face. I was telling myself the bullshit stories surrounding working out and convincing myself that this behaviour was helping me and driving me to a better place.

It wasn't; it was the complete opposite, exposing many other problems in my life. I found myself being led into eating disorders, massive binge eating episodes, and food addictions. All this fuelled even more emotion-suppressing workouts, and the steep downward spiral continued.

Our bodies are not designed to sit on the couch or at a desk all day. They are born to move, made to run, sprint, and walk, not sit down ALL day. If we are not doing this, our bodies start to shut down and eliminate the parts we are not using. A broken arm is placed in a cast for 6-8 weeks, and when the cast is finally removed, you often see that the healed arm has shrunk due to the muscles' lack of use. Just as the saying goes, if you don't use it, you lose it.

I recently saw an article that showed a man's upper thigh at the ages of 35, 50 and 85. You could see the decline in the muscle-to-fat ratio over the period. The study was to show muscle differences over time when they are not used. At 35, the muscle made up 90% of the leg and had a thin strip of fat around the outside. At age 85, the muscle had shrunk to around 20-30% of total leg mass, with fat making up most of it. It was quite unbelievable to see.[33]

## Weaponise Your Body

That is why we all treat our bodies as if they are a weapon. This weapon works as an accelerator, guiding you on your journey to become the ultimate fully functional man that you can be. When it comes to weaponising your body, the first step in this journey is to work out every day. This doesn't mean you must go to the gym to score for the day. Working out can be as simple as going for a walk or a jog, going for a surf, skating, or playing a team sport. It's not important what the exercise is, as long as it is something.

Many men think fitness is an all-or-nothing pursuit, and you have to either commit to working out hard every day or not at all. The thing about fitness is there are 1000s of ways to get it and, more importantly, 1000s of ways to make it enjoyable. We have several ways in which we can provide fitness for our bodies.

1. Pick up something heavy a few times

2. Pick up something moderately heavy lots of times

3. Endurance work: running, swimming, cycling, rowing, and long walks.

4. Sprinting

5. Through a hobby which you enjoy. Golf, biking, skating, surfing, tennis, basketball, etc.

Treat your body as if you are an athlete, even if you have no desire to be one, which I'm guessing you don't want to be anyway. The more you think and act the way an athlete would, the more your mind and body will adapt to consider yourself an athlete.

## What Would an Athlete Do?

It doesn't take much to look around the different societies we live in and see the men who are running at 50% and those who are running a bit higher at 80%. You will rarely see a man running at 100% capacity, jumping out of bed in the morning, and feeling like a god.

There's a story of a lady who lost a ridiculous amount of weight by simply asking herself this one question in every situation, 'what would a fitness pro do?' This small shift started to change the way she saw things and the habits she had formed. If she was at the counter ordering food, 'what would a fitness pro do?', so she ordered a salad. When she got to the stairs, 'what would a fitness pro do?', so she took the stairs instead of the lift. From now on, remind yourself that you have the choice to do 'what an athlete would do' and see how drastically your life can change.

I say with full confidence that if you follow this, you will enjoy and prosper in this new way of living that will fundamentally shift your life to places you never thought possible.

## KEY POINTS

**POINT #1:** This body, YOUR body, is the only one you will ever get.

**POINT #2:** It generally takes something bad to happen to our bodies for us to wake up to the fact that we have been neglecting them.

**POINT #3:** You cannot build and lead as a man if you get out of breath from walking up two sets of stairs.

**POINT #4:** You cannot have passionate sex if you only get in 30 seconds before you need a break.

**POINT #5:** You cannot desire to build anything great if all you want to do is sit on the couch, eat pizza, drink beer, and watch TV.

**POINT #6:** This is not about turning you into an athlete, nor is it about turning you into a gym junkie or CrossFit groupie. The principle is simple, your body and your fitness level are the gateways to your power and energy.

**POINT #7:** Our bodies are not designed to sit on the couch or at a desk all day. They are born to move, made to run, sprint, and walk, not sit down ALL day.

**POINT #8:** Adopting this habit will allow you to l enjoy and prosper in a new way of living that will fundamentally shift your life to places you never thought possible.

# 28

## THE DAILY 8: #2

### SMOOTHIE

*"Looking good and feeling good go hand in hand. If you have a healthy lifestyle, your diet and nutrition are set, and you're working out, you're going to feel good."*
**- Jason Statham**

How you see food directly impacts the power you produce and the energy output you have available. I am honestly still so surprised at the lack of knowledge, thought, and even care that men give to the shit they just shovel into their mouths. Only to end up overweight, with high cholesterol, diabetes, or other internal organ problems and think, *'How did that happen?'*. If you fall into any of these categories, there's only one person responsible for that: you. You're the one that got yourself in this situation, which means you are also the one who can get yourself out.

During my time working and living in camp accommodation throughout Australia, every meal supplied in these camps was a full-on buffet. For some men inside these camps, breakfast, lunch, and dinner was treated as an all-you-can-eat-feast-fest. Seconds, thirds, even fourths for some, and I haven't even started on dessert yet. No sign of self-control and not a thought is given while they were piling that shit in. I realised that a man's mindset and how he interprets food are skewed.

At some stage during this period, when I was working away FIFO, I became so obsessed with training and nutrition that I was studying and consuming every bit of information I could at any opportunity. I would look at these men and get stressed out, thinking, 'they're crossing this nutrient with this macro-nutrient, which will release Y chemical that will have X effect on their body.' I was completely overcomplicating it.

### The Over-Complication of Food

There are a thousand diets and also a thousand different ways to overcomplicate food and nutrition. Before any healthy foundation is built, people begin by focusing on the smallest things that really don't make much difference. Every new guru on the block is looking for the next best hack or shortcut to set them apart. The reality is that it's the basics that work, and the basics have always worked and will continue to work.

A simple detail of life is that we need three things to survive, food, water, and nutrients. But how we view the food we eat can vary from man to man. You can view food as fuel. You can view food as a short-term reward. You can view food as an enemy like people with eating disorders do, or you can view food as a social experience. There's no right and wrong way you should view food; it's your view, but the principle is simple: if you don't fill up with the right stuff consistently, you are in trouble.

For you to get the greatest benefit from your nutrition and greatness, which is what we strive for within AMD, you will have to change a few things around food as you currently see and know it. How are you fuelling your Ferrari?[34] Are you fuelling a Ferrari, or are you fuelling a beat-up old Ford Falcon? Your body and physique might not be at the standard of a Ferrari, but if you fuel it with shit, it will run shit. When you fuel it with premium fuels, it will start to improve, and it will start to transform into the level and standard of a Ferrari.

## Cleaning Under the Hood

Each morning when we fuel our bodies with this green smoothie goodness, we are flushing out all the toxins that have been built up and stored over time. It's not until our bodies purge out these toxins that we feel the full effect of the green smoothies. Removing these toxins from the digestive track actually affects how you feel, how you function, and how you think. The gut is known as the second brain.

When you remove these toxins, your body can process and move food/ waste faster under the hood, which is why you'll become fitter, leaner, and ultimately feel better. When you feel better, you do more, and when you do more, you become more. When you become more, you have more.

So right now, the focus isn't about telling you what you can't have or what you have to subtract or remove from your diet. We are simply adding this one thing every morning; a green drink or smoothie every single day.

## The Constant Food Baby

Before starting down this daily smoothie path a few years back, I was constantly bloated after eating a meal. I would never be completely full and satisfied. I'd eat a lot of food and be physically full, but my stomach would be telling me to eat more. I would eat, walk around for an hour or two with a bloated food baby, and then come good a few hours later. Only to repeat that cycle the next time I ate. I could not work out what was happening inside my body.

I thought I might have food intolerances or that something just wasn't agreeing with me. I studied more and more, which was probably the worst thing I could have done. I bought different new-age hippy teas, powdered clays, and bucket loads of tablets — all things I thought might help me, but they didn't do anything.

I decided to stop trying to self-diagnose and instead went to the local doctors. After a 30-minute conversation, the only answers I got were to drink more water and eat more vegetables. *'Are you kidding me? That's the only answer you have?'* Doc, I need more than that.

It was around that time when a bodybuilder I had been following for a few years, Ben Pakulski, gave a link in an email to an eBook called *101 Juicing Recipes*[35] (actual juice, not steroids). I don't know who put this list together, but I went all in. As I do with most things, I always dive straight in and get the best I can. I got that from my father. So, I went out and bought a $900 slow press juicer that took close to 30 minutes to make one juice and about the same amount of time to clean up.

My first juice wasn't enjoyable, but I forced it down. Nothing much happened at first, but after a week, my body had never been the same. I felt 30kg lighter and had an unstoppable amount of energy. Within a week, I had fixed my bloating problem, which had been messing with my body for a least a year by that stage.

## Smoothie Refinement

Over the years, I have refined my smoothie game, switching between this extravagant cold press operation, supplements, store-bought juices, and now to my nutria-ninja. I've never felt better on the inside, and I'm in the best shape of my life, leaner, fitter, and stronger than ever before. I even recently signed a deal to be sponsored by a supplement company. My body is a weapon, and my mind is clearer than it ever has been. All because of the addition of a green smoothie to my diet. I struggled for years trying to get to this place because I thought I needed to keep eating less and eating smaller meals. The reality is that I needed to eat more and add fuel to my body. The same thing may be true for you.

A lot of people's mindset has been based on the belief that achieving the fitness level they want, the body they desire, and the right diet program to suit their needs is accomplished only by subtraction. This leads people to create an internal prison around food, which is widely prevalent in the health and fitness industry. Constant obsessions around food, eating disorders, binge eating, and yoyo weight-loss diets are all outcomes of when people try to subtract foods/fuels from their lives. I, for one, was one of those people.

This mentality of subtraction doesn't work; it amplifies the feeling of 'want' and 'lack' while creating scarcity. As soon as you tell yourself to limit something, your mind is automatically attracted to it. When a man doesn't have much money, he wants more. When a man hasn't had sex for a while, he thinks about it and wants it more. When a man tells himself he can't have a doughnut, he thinks about eating that doughnut a lot more.

As I mentioned previously, I recently completed Andy Frisella's 75HARD Mental Toughness Challenge.[36] If you haven't heard of this, it's where you have to do 5 things for a total of 75 days. #3 is you must commit to a diet. No cheat days, no alcohol/drugs and no days off.

Before this, I never told myself I couldn't eat anything but always eat clean and healthy; I never felt like eating crap.

As soon as I started 75HARD and knew I couldn't have anything that wasn't in my diet, something strange happened. I would walk through the supermarket and be craving all the stuff I couldn't have. I'd drive past McDonalds and think it would be nice to have that. I haven't had Maccas in years, and it's the last thing I would want to eat. The only reason I wanted it was because I knew I couldn't. This just goes to show why so many diets fail when self-imposed food restrictions are put in place.

## Add Not Subtract

How is it possible that in the society we currently live in, with the ever-expanding knowledge and consistent levels of studies being undertaken, the population is getting fatter and fatter every year? You don't have to be a rocket scientist to realise that the current focus on subtracting calories instead of adding nutrients is not working.

Now, I can't take credit for this. Of course, green smoothies have been around for years now. What I can take credit for is that I have religiously woken up, completed some kind of workout, and then pounded as much frozen spinach into my nutria-ninja as possible, along with a few other things. I know that adding this to your morning will not only give your body a massive nutrient hit and a massive easing of the digestive tract, but you will start to see a shift in your body composition. Especially if you currently have eating habits similar to those mentioned at the start of this chapter.

## Understanding of Food

I love food, I love tasty food, and I'm sure you do too, but this doesn't mean that every meal has to be enjoyable. For some reason, we have become dependent on food to be a big social event or based our social lives around this concept of eating a full-on MasterChef-inspired dinner. Or even going to a restaurant for dinner every night.

The mindset that we want to build here is that eating is fuel. Sometimes, it will be fun; other times, it will just be fuel. In doing this, we shift the mindset or mentality that food isn't the part that creates the fun within the setting. It's the people and the company we are around.

There have been plenty of times when I have gone to dinner with friends and family but have not eaten. I ate at home before I went so that I wouldn't get sucked into the trap of ordering the special of the day plus two sides plates plus an entrée, all high-calorie dense meals, which so often happens when men eat out.

This was a concept that was hard to grip for many of the friends I went out with. I would always get questioned about why I would bother coming to dinner if I wasn't going to eat. They were all stuck in this mindset that food is the fun and that food is the reason for the outing. This has nothing to do with my friends, who I love to death. This is just the mentality of nearly everybody you and I know and will ever meet. You can only change YOUR mindset and YOUR mentality around this, so be prepared for the questions and the lack of understanding from others.

This isn't an overnight change, nor will you wake up tomorrow with a new belief toward food. This is a daily, consistent shift in your journey to fuelling your Ferrari, and it could take 3 or 4 years for you to reach Ferrari status.

Nothing is complicated with a green smoothie. This is no magic trick, nor is it some new hype. This shit works. You can do all the research you like. There are thousands of studies and references out there around the effectiveness that this addition has on your body and your life.

Stop worrying about all the food you shouldn't be eating or don't want to, and shift your focus to the foods you *are* eating. The green smoothie is one of them. Green smoothies work by detoxifying your body and releasing the extra muck and associated bloating that's trapped inside you, leaving you feeling lighter, leaner, and functioning more efficiently.

Here, we will get a point each day for this new addition to your life: your green smoothie. Don't just make it a habit; make it something your body craves and cannot go without each morning. I can tell you from my own experiences that missing just one day greatly impacts how I feel and function for that day.

## KEY POINTS

**POINT #1:** How you see food directly impacts the power you produce and the energy output you have available.

**POINT #2:** There are a thousand diets and also a thousand different ways to overcomplicate food and nutrition. Before any healthy foundation is built, people begin by focusing on the smallest things that really don't make much difference.

**POINT #3:** How are you fuelling your Ferrari? Are you fuelling a Ferrari, or are you fuelling a beat-up old Ford Falcon?

**POINT #4:** The mindset that we want to build here is that eating is fuel. Sometimes, it will be fun; other times, it will just be fuel.

**POINT #5:** Each morning when we fuel our bodies with this green smoothie goodness, we are flushing out all the toxins that have been built up and stored over time.

**POINT #6:** They work by detoxifying your body and releasing the extra muck and associated bloating that's trapped inside you, leaving you feeling lighter, leaner, and functioning more efficiently.

**POINT #7:** Don't just make it a habit; make it something your body craves and cannot go without each morning.

# 29

## THE DAILY 8: #3

### GCGS

*"Develop an attitude of gratitude, and give thanks for everything that happens to you, knowing that every step forward is a step toward achieving something bigger and better than your current situation."*
- **Brian Tracy**

I wouldn't be the first person to say that you should set goals, and I definitely won't be the last. But the whole goal-setting 'process' that people are trying to convince others of makes this process much more complicated than it needs to be.

We have so-called 'gurus' teaching us how to set goals, make SMART goals, clearly defined goals, or whatever other new term is getting thrown around right now. These so-called experts show and teach people how to set goals, but that's as far as it goes. You can see why so many of these goals do not become a reality.

No matter how SMART or clearly defined a goal, there is no guarantee that this goal will be completed. If you don't know what SMART is short for, it's Specific, Measurable, Attainable, Realistic and Timely. This is where it goes wrong. If 92% of people don't reach their goals and there's no guarantee that this goal will happen.[37] Why do people continue to set goals that are realistic and attainable? Clearly, they are not attainable, are they?

Why don't we use that to our advantage and make our goals purposely unattainable? Let's use money as it's an easy example; let's say your goal was to make 10k per month. So you start doing what you need to do to make that happen. 92% of the time it won't happen mind you. Stick with me here.

Instead, what if we make that goal 100k per month. All of a sudden, you're asking yourself a question, what would I have to do to make 100k per month? What's happening here is your ceiling of possibility has grown, and your thinking is bigger. Your focus is on making 100k, not 10k. That small little 10k target seems small compared to your 100k target. More often than not, you'll blast past the 10k target a lot quicker. So let's shorten SMART to SMT and kick out the Realistic and Attainable. That's for people who are settling for average.

Setting goals goes deeper than just setting goals, and I want to introduce you to a different way of thinking about your goals.

## A Goal Is No More Than A Dream

Hear me out, and I'll explain. Most people have some sort of goal they want to achieve, whether it be around health and fitness, career, wealth creation, relationships, or anything in between. The perfect example is New Year's Resolutions. Most of these 'new year, new me' goals don't even last a month before they are given up.

As I mentioned earlier, science says that 92% of people don't achieve their goals. However, everyone is still focused on setting them. If this isn't the definition of insanity, then I don't know what is.

## G – Goal/Target

That is why we teach inside the MMC not to set goals but to set targets. Just like a bullseye target in a shooting range, targets are designed to be hit. Not only do we design them in a way that allows them to be hit, but we also quantify the rate at which they are hit tenfold by adding a series of benchmarks along the way to ensure success.

We have daily targets, weekly targets, monthly targets, quarterly targets, and yearly targets. We will discuss and break these down in further detail in the last chapter.

When you think of a bullseye target, the first ring around the outside is like your daily targets. If you hit it just once, it won't equate to much, and you won't move mountains. But if you hit that every single day with your GCGs, your points will slowly add up. Rome wasn't built in a day, just like the life of your dreams won't be.

This is the beginning of your daily documenting inside the King's Journal. So, we start by writing down your target for that particular day. Don't worry about the bigger targets; just aim to hit that outside ring of the bullseye target. It's been proven many times that people who write down their goals are much more likely to achieve them.

Although writing your targets down won't magically mean they are hit, these statements send the power of your unconscious mind on a mission to find solutions to fulfil your targets. You might not know the exact steps to take immediately, but by allowing yourself time to ponder and trusting that your mind will find the answers, these will soon become clear.

### Finding Your Elephant

This concept is why I'm constantly smashing my targets, which may have seemed impossible to the man I was when I first set them. Although I know they will not seem impossible to the man I will be in 12 months when these targets are accomplished. It all starts from that one daily target that one statement to yourself that this is your target for the day, and this one thing will be your bite of the elephant.

Early on in my journey, I was listening to an audiobook. It told a story about a drunk entrepreneur who was talking to one of his admirers. The conversation was about business, productivity and tackling big tasks. The drunk entrepreneur leaned over at one point and said, 'kid, how do you eat an elephant?'. The answer was 'One bite at a time.'

### One Bite At A Time

This thing had stuck with me ever since that day when I first heard it. This is exactly why we set impossible targets for 12 months. Right now, they might seem like we're trying to eat an elephant. After committing to a daily target designed to direct you toward this impossible end goal, you take your one bite for the day. That one daily bite will take that target from impossibility to the place of achievability.

### C – Commitment

I want to start by saying that this commitment has nothing to do with anyone but you. Unless you openly state your commitment for the day, nobody will ever know what you have set for that day. This isn't a matter of trying to just get it done or do the minimum you need to get it done. It's a matter of doing the work and doing your best. Live by the 4 Laws.

## Don't Let Yourself Down

Once you commit to yourself, you are the only person you are letting down if you don't stick to it. Not your partner or spouse, not your sons or daughters, not your parents or siblings, not your boss or workmates, only yourself. At the end of the day, no one else *really* cares about it apart from yourself. The problem with this is that we don't care if we let ourselves down. We'll probably go spin another BS story around why we didn't get something done or how we can make it up tomorrow.

So, this is where your realness and ability to tell the truth come into play. I don't care; your family doesn't care, and nobody cares if you complete your commitments or not. Which begs the question, why bother? Why bother even completing this if nobody cares?

The answer lies within you. If you cannot commit to yourself, how will you ever commit to anyone else? How you do one thing is how you do everything. If you are unwilling to do something, don't commit to doing it and just not do it. That is the definition of lying. There's nothing wrong with not committing or not wanting to commit. What is wrong is committing to something knowing you are going to break that commitment.

Although I've said several times nobody cares if you are true to your commitments to yourself, everybody will be able to tell. The results will show the facts about your commitments.

This is a hard pill to swallow, and it was especially hard for me to swallow after my first real relationship break-up. It exposed the shell of the 'boy' I was and the lack of commitment I showed to this relationship. I was covering up and hiding the truth about my commitments, which I knew deep down I wasn't staying true to. I didn't realise it was in plain sight for everyone else to see.

I would expect her to do everything for me, but I didn't provide anything in return. I would commit to doing something only to turn around and make up some excuse not to do it because I just didn't want to. As honest and ashamed as I can be, my biggest lack of commitment and my biggest lie was when it came to my workmates. I would tell them she was just a 'friend with benefits,' knowing all too well that we were in a committed relationship.

### Commitments Show Up

The commitments you make every day, or the lack of commitments you make, will show no matter how much you try and cover them up. No matter how unimportant you think they are or how you think you will be able to catch up with them tomorrow. Like me and that first relationship I was in, you will eventually be exposed for not being real, raw, and honest inside the commitments you choose or choose not to make.

So, we have the G, the goal/target you set for that particular day you want to achieve, which can be a daily, weekly, or monthly target. And just now, we have added the C. A commitment, a written statement of what you will not be going to sleep without completing.

I've had men say, 'I don't have any targets right now' or 'I don't have any targets I can work on every day'. Let me tell you that that is not true. After you've understood what it is to live by the MMC, you will have targets that you will set. This can be as simple as G – I want to lose 2kg/5lbs, or C – I'm committed to not eating dessert after dinner. See how easy this is. Don't worry about your targets being big or solving worldwide problems; don't listen to this hype around goal-setting. Set targets, and hit targets with daily commitments. Save your bigger, less attainable (remember SMT) goals for your 1, 2 and 5-year goals.

## G – Gratitude

This is similar to your daily gratitude text, which, again, we'll discuss in an upcoming chapter. Instead, we are just opening up our awareness around the simple things that are often taken for granted.

The first time I experienced this was when I was with my first girlfriend on my first overseas trip. Yes, the same one I just spoke about who I was telling everyone we were fuck-buddies. We went to the island of Fiji, a beautiful, beautiful place. This was the first time I experienced what poverty was actually like. After now seeing 38 countries around the world, Fiji definitely isn't the worst place I've seen. Still, it's just normal life for these people.

I can remember driving from the airport to our hotel thinking, 'How do these people live like this?' and 'How can these people be laughing and looking like they are having so much fun? As I sit here now, looking back at this experience, I realise that the local Fijians are some of the happiest people on earth, which is the case for so many people in third-world countries.[38] They have so little but also so much.

Now, you can't change where you are born or raised or the reality you are exposed to, but you can change your attitude and gratitude for the things you do have. Practising gratitude daily allows you to expend all this positive energy while allowing positive energy to be reflected back to you.

### Changing Brain Chemistry

Just asking the question 'What am I grateful for?' has the ability to change the chemistry inside your brain.[39] Even if you can't think of anything to be grateful for at that moment, you will still get this shift in chemistry. During the times when you might be finding it hard to be able to see anything to be grateful for, there's always something to be grateful for. The food we eat, the water we drink, the roof over our heads or the bed we sleep in.

The real power in this comes when you allow yourself to be grateful for the struggles you are experiencing in your life. I mean truly gratefully, not just saying, 'yes, I'm grateful for this struggle' only to think moments later, 'why does this always happen to me?'. There are two ways to look at everything that happens for you. I say for you as life is happening *for* you, not *to* you. So, you can sit there feeling sorry for yourself as a victim, or you can express gratitude towards this situation and treat what has happened as a gift.

*'Each of these situations has two outcomes. Either you can see it as an opportunity for growth, or see it as an obstacle that will hinder your growth ability. You ultimately get to choose.'* – Wayne Dyer.

Be grateful for the ability to do the things you do. Many men have a long list of things they think they *have* to do. I *have* to go to work. I *have* to cook dinner. I *have* to go to the gym. By adopting a perspective of gratitude, you experience a small shift in context that creates a massive difference in perception. This shift turns 'I *have* to do X' into 'I *get* to do X.'; I get the chance to do all those things.

### Graduate Towards Struggles

Around the time I first started implementing GCGs religiously in my life, I had three credit card debts and two other smaller loans that I was paying off. Every day for a few months, I would write down the words 'I'm grateful for being humbled by not having any money', 'I'm grateful for having these struggles that will require me to grow to get out of them', 'I'm grateful for the needs to be better and do better, and to grow more to overcome my struggles.'

I was taken right back down to earth every morning when I wrote this. It removed my little ego from everything I did and left me in a place of humbleness for that day. Being thankful for my struggles allowed me to enjoy the positive experiences so much more and shift the focus away from the pain I had felt. Allowing positive thinking in will open your eyes to more opportunities.

This is why we add the practice of gratitude to this equation. Adding gratitude to this powerful daily tool is the perfect way to round off your daily GCGs. The individual impact of one day of expressing gratitude may be small, but the cumulative effect is huge, and you'll begin to realise that nearly every day is a good day, in a small way at the very least.

So, to recap our three steps:

**Step #1:** G – Write down your goal or target for that particular day.

**Step #2:** C – Declare your commitment for that day, which aligns with the goal or target you are working to achieve.

**Step #3:** G – Express gratitude for something in your life.

## KEY POINTS

**POINT #1:** G = Goal/Target

- Science says that 92% of people don't achieve their goals.

- Let's use that to our advantage and purposefully set them to be unattainable.

- Shorten SMART Goals to SMT Goals and kick out the Realistic and Attainable.

**POINT #2:** C = Commitment

- Once you commit to yourself, you are the only person you are letting down if you don't stick to it.

- If you cannot commit to yourself, how will you ever commit to anyone else? How you do one thing is how you do everything.

- If you are unwilling to do something, don't commit to doing it and just not do it.

**POINT #3:** G = Gratitude

- Just asking the question 'What am I grateful for?' has the ability to change the chemistry inside your brain.

- The real power in this comes when you allow yourself to be grateful for the struggles you are experiencing in your life.

**POINT #4:** So, to recap our three steps:

**Step #1:** G – Write down your goal or target for that particular day.

**Step #2:** C – Declare your commitment for that day, which aligns with the goal or target you are working to achieve.

**Step #3:** G – Express gratitude for something in your life.

# 30

## THE DAILY 8: #4

### READING

*"Everything we do is for the purpose of altering consciousness. We form friendships so that we can feel certain emotions, like love, and avoid others, like loneliness. We eat specific foods to enjoy their fleeting presence on our tongues. We read for the pleasure of thinking another person's thoughts."*
**- Sam Harris**

This is no new concept; this is not a new 'fad' that has just emerged. Undoubtedly, reading positively impacts your life, who you are, and who you want to become. I can tell you about countless well-known men who said it all started with a single book. I can also tell you about countless numbers of well-known men who read for hours daily.

Reading for a minimum of 30 minutes daily is the next addition to the Daily 8. If you are sitting there thinking, 'I am already reading,' that's great. You're in the minority of men. But are you getting the maximum impact from the time you spend reading? This component might not be an addition for you but rather a shift in the direction of what you are reading and consuming. What you are reading is far more important than just the act of reading.

The concept around time and the 'lack of time' bullshit excuses I hear from men not having time to read for just 30 minutes per day. Ok, so let's look at the facts of time; 2 hours and 22 minutes is the average time someone spends on social media daily. 12 minutes a day is the average time someone spends waiting to catch public transport. 22 minutes a day is the average time spent waiting for a meal to be prepared at a restaurant, and 10 minutes a day is the average time spent waiting in line for the post office.[40] Lastly, 70 minutes a week is the average time men spend watching porn.[41] Depending on when you are reading this, those numbers could be higher.

We let time pass by us every day without so much as a thought. I don't think most men fully realise how limited their time is and that it's gone for good once it's gone. However, time is not the issue here; it's the unwillingness and the inability to see how this can impact a man's life. Most fail to make any decision regarding this, so all they do is just let the days roll on by and unfold before them. Again, time is not the issue, and it's not an excuse that will fly here.

### Passing Time Myth

The point of this chapter isn't about the importance of time, but I'm glad we made it here. It's a conversation that needs to be had with the ever-growing use of the term 'I'm just passing the time.' Make the most of your time here as a human experience on this magical planet and enjoy what little time you have. I used to be guilty of doing things to pass the time, and I think every man has been. Take it from me, a man who has passed the time and wished away some of the best years of my life while doing things I wasn't enjoying: make the most of what you have.

When I first started the habit of reading daily – before I had developed the Daily 8 – I had only one part of the day when I was able to read. Reading before bed would put me to sleep after a long day working a physical job. At the same time, in the mornings, I'd lose concentration and struggle to read without my mind drifting off. The one time left to me was smoko – a construction slang term used for morning tea. During the ten years I worked in the construction industry, I did not once see anyone pick up a book during their break. Not a single person! And I worked on jobs with hundreds of different workers.

As you can imagine, I got all sorts of reactions: questions about why I was reading the books, comments telling me that it wouldn't help me and that it was just a load of crap. Everyone had their own opinion, and everyone wanted to tell me how I should and should not be living my life based on what I was reading. So, when I hear the excuse that I don't have time or don't have anywhere to read, I realise that it actually comes down to the fact that they just don't want to read. By the time you reach the end of this chapter, you will not only understand why it's so beneficial for you to adopt this Daily 8 habit, but you'll actually want to be reading more than the suggested 30 minutes a day.

It all starts with personal growth, which by far is the most important thing you can do on your journey. Sadly, it is non-existent in the lives of so many men. This desire to constantly improve yourself and aspire to become better is the whole basis of what AMD is built upon. To improve your life and the lives of people you come in contact with, aka the ripple effect. Dedicate this time, these 30 minutes of reading, to learning something related to personal growth. Whether it's a book on finance, self-development, entrepreneurship, self-help, business, investing, or whatever else you decide you need to become better. I'm not talking about reading about history, geography, or anything alike. That has its place, but it doesn't count towards the Daily 8 reading score.

### The 1% Rule

What if you were able to improve yourself by just 1% every day? Twenty minutes a day equates to 1% of your day. If we were to get better by reading something that allows us to improve our abilities inside these 20 minutes, we would reach that status of being 1% better. Having 30 minutes to read allows for any shortfalls and maximises our full 20 minutes of learning. This small daily shift can guide your life to a whole new destination and can be the difference between who you are and who you could be.

1% doesn't sound like much on its own, but when you compound that daily 1% improvement, that's when you start to see results. After just one year, you are actually 37.78% better. That's a 37.78% better you in only one year, and it's basic maths.[42] This type of improvement is shown in a man, in how he looks, in how he carries himself, in the income he earns, and by the people he associates with.

Simply 20 minutes a day can change your life in just one year. How many people in your life, whether it be family members, friends, or workmates, who you see each and every year doing the same thing they always have. They are no further advanced than they were in the previous five years and will probably be in the exact same spot in another five years. This is because they have not decided to invest time and resources into their own personal growth.

I can remember a couple of times at the start where I hadn't been able to get in my daily reading, sometimes for a few days in a row, and I actually felt dumber. This might sound strange, but I can tell you my ability to think and communicate begins to decline after just a few days. My productivity, thinking and creativity also suffer.

Through reading, men gain new life perspectives and learn more about themselves and the world around them. With new perspectives come new possibilities. Reading the books and scriptures of others can be so powerful in your quest to become the best version you can be. There is a wealth of knowledge out there, and experts have dedicated their whole life to their chosen field. You can access that expert's life's work in just one small book. You can learn from the life experience and mistakes of others that could save you years of figuring it out on your own.

### Raising Your Awareness

Not only are you constantly getting 1% better as you consume this content, but a number of things are also going on beneath the surface. Reading is the best way to increase exposure to new words and learn how to use them in context. Awareness of these words increases your ability to use them whenever you feel fit. Reading about other people can help you understand people better, which is a big proponent of effective communication. Books allow you to roam through the world, travel back in time, and look to the future, providing you with a deeper understanding of ideas, concepts, practices, emotions, and events. Reading can open your awareness to new options that you may not have known about or considered before. We can then share all of these with others during our conversations.

For a long time in my life, I thought reading was a waste of time and believed that all it did was put me to sleep. Because of this, when I would start to read, my mind would begin preparing for sleep. It was not that the act of reading was putting me to sleep but that I had told my mind to put me to sleep every time I read. The additional problem was that I probably wasn't reading about things that interested me.

I can honestly say that this particular Daily 8 habit is the one I wish I had started earlier. I don't regret it because I might not be where I am in my life, doing what I'm doing, had I not followed this exact course of events. Still, it's definitely something that I wish I could have started sooner. Having said that, it's still not too late to start. It's never too late to start anything, for that matter.

There's a common misconception about learning and taking in what we consume that comes directly from our schooling. We try to learn the stuff required at school, but it never seems to stick in our heads. Why is that? Why is learning made so hard? The simple fact is that we don't truly care what we are learning about. Information is forced upon us in order to pass a particular subject. I'm sure you've experienced the same thing, sitting in class trying to learn something. In the back of your mind, you're thinking, 'Why am I learning this?' or 'When am I ever going to need any of this in life?' — think algebra.

Having completed 12 or so years of schooling plus any further college or university studies, we enter the real world with those same principles shaping our learning abilities. Meanwhile, the idea of any learning beyond this is dismissed. This Daily 8 habit is different; when you are fully interested in the subject or item you are educating yourself about, the information you consume is implanted in the front of your mind. This is why I'm not giving you any books to read. Do your research, and find books that truly interest you and will allow you to reach that 1% improved benchmark.

### Don't Be Afraid To Stop

If you don't like the book or it is not what you thought it would be about, stop reading it. Just because you started doesn't mean you have to struggle through just to finish it. You're far better off starting a different one of greater interest to you at that particular time. I have started reading books only to get a few chapters in and decide they weren't a good fit for me. I end up putting them back on my bookshelf to read later when they might be more appealing to my state of mind.

Make up your own mind on what you choose to read; don't just go with a top 10 must-read list you happen to find on Google. I realised fairly quickly that everyone is quick to give you a book recommendation, but half of them won't be of any interest to you. I still haven't read the first three books I bought from recommendations, and they are still sitting on my bookshelf, collecting dust. So make sure you do your research and find the best ones that suit you at that time.

This concludes the Daily 8 chapter for reading. 30 minutes a day on a personal growth subject of your choice equates to a 1% better you and therefore gives you 1 point in the Daily 8 game.

## KEY POINTS

**POINT #1:** Reading positively impacts your life, who you are, and who you want to become.

**POINT #2:** There's no surprise that most successful people read daily.

**POINT #3:** Reading for a minimum of 30 minutes daily is the next addition to the Daily 8.

**POINT #4:** Dedicate this time to learning something related to personal growth. Whether it's a book on finance, self-development, entrepreneurship, self-help, business, investing, or whatever else you decide you need to become better.

**POINT #5:** Twenty minutes a day equates to 1% of your day. If we were to get better by reading something that allows us to improve our abilities within these 20 minutes, we would reach that status of being 1% better.

**POINT #6:** When you compound that daily 1% improvement, after just one year, you are actually 37.78% better. That's a 37.78% better you in only one year.

# 31

## THE DAILY 8: #5

### TEXT MESSAGES

*"Happiness cannot be traveled to, owned, earned, worn or consumed. Happiness is the spiritual experience of living every minute with love, grace, and gratitude."*
**- Denis Waitley**

Sending a simple text message. We are not talking about sending just any old random message. More than likely, there are already many sent and received on your mobile phone every day. We're talking about a specifically designed message with a strategic strategy through which you can make your daily instalment.

## Strategic Deposits

Let me explain how this all began. I walked home from the third day of a five-day event I had travelled halfway across the world to attend. Still, to this day, I'm not sure exactly why I was there, and I just had the feeling that I needed to go.

At the end of that third day, all the attendees were invited to send a video message expressing our gratitude to five different people in our lives. Instantly, I started to construct some kind of justification as to why I shouldn't have to do it and that it wouldn't make any difference. Trying to justify these stories is a waste of my time and effort.

Amongst all the chaos and stress that flooded my mind, one thing was getting louder and louder. As much as I kept reiterating these reasons and talking myself out of sending these videos, there was that voice again that wouldn't go away. It wouldn't let up on telling me to send those messages.

It sounds like such a simple task, but at the time, I was so nervous at the thought of filming these stupid little videos, or what I thought were stupid at the time. 'What was I going to say?' 'What am I thankful for?' 'How are they going to respond?' I started with my mother, 'what am I thanking her for?'. My hands started to shake, and I could feel my heart beating from the inside. It felt like the time in grade five when I had to speak in front of the class, but I was shaking so much that it seemed like I was shivering.

Thinking back on it now, it seems like such a little minute task for the man I am today. I can't explain how hard it was for me that evening to flip my camera around, look at my reflection staring back at me, and tell the people around me, 'thank you for everything you have done for me, thank you for pulling me in line, thank you for believing in me when I didn't, thank you for being there for me. I respect you, and I love you.'

It was late in the evening when I was walking home filming these videos. After many attempts to say what I wanted, I had completed all five videos and sent them off. I sent them off and turned my phone off straight away, trying to delay the time it would be until I saw the responses. I woke up to see that the messages had been sent back to me with a similar response. All it took was for me to send a message like that in order to get one in return.

This one message changed the way I saw myself, and it changed the way I viewed relationships. I began to notice the people around me who had wonderful relationships with their parents, siblings, wives/ girlfriends, and friends. All this external noise was distracting me from what I had available in my own life. Living in the story that it just is what it is. Some guys have good relationships, and others don't. Why is this? Why was I not experiencing the relationships that I wanted? And why did I find it so hard to send those messages that night?

As the weeks went by, I couldn't stop thinking about the whole experience I'd had sending those videos. It was like I started to connect that little bit more after just this one message. If I send messages like this more often, I thought to myself, I wonder what results I would see.

### 'I Appreciate You'

Twelve months later, I had been seeing this girl on and off for a few months, and I decided it was time for me to really test this out and send her a video. 'What should I say to her?' I sat there for a few minutes, trying to think of something. I was stuck. I didn't want to say something lame like, 'Thanks for hanging out with me' or, 'Thanks for being you' or anything else. 'Tell her why you appreciate her' was my suggestion from within. So that's what I did. I told her exactly why I appreciated her.

One minute passed, five minutes passed, one hour went by, and still no reply. I could see the little tick in the corner of the message indicating that she'd seen it. 'What had I done! Good one, Brendon, you just stuffed that one up'.

It wasn't until the next day that she sent a video back to me saying a very similar thing. In that video, she mentioned that it took her so long to reply because it made her cry every time she tried. Here I was, assuming that I had said something that didn't go down well. This was back when I wasn't living true to Pillar #3 – Assume Nothing.

The next time we met, our whole relationship changed, and I looked at her in a completely different way. We connected on a much deeper level, and it felt like a light had been lit between the both of us. I had no idea and had never been taught how relationships work, leading me to constantly be unsure how to approach things. If there were something I felt or wanted to say, I either would lie about it or just not say anything at all.

After a few weeks, I could see that light was slowly starting to fade away. So, I decided to do the same again. This time the thought came through, 'Tell her why you respect her,' and that's what I did. This time there was no reply, but it didn't bother me at all. I knew she had watched it, and I felt great on the inside for doing it. The light once again turned up its intensity.

### Keeping the Light Lit

Knowing the power of sending just one of these videos and experiencing their almost instant effect, I pondered over the impact regular videos would have on keeping this fire strong. What if I could send one each week? So, every Sunday, I would decide what I wanted to say, film it and send it off. I wouldn't get a reply, and I was ok with that. In the end, this message wasn't about me. It was for the person on the other end. I knew the light inside my relationship would stay lit as long as I kept sending these videos.

Over the next few months, I experimented with sending videos more and more often. Eventually, this simple act became what we now know inside the Daily 8 as a small text message daily.

Every morning I wake up, and every morning I send a message, along with the other Daily 8 elements inside the MMC. I choose a relationship I want to work on; sometimes, it would be the same person every day, or it would be someone different. I'd select from one of the three areas, respect, gratitude, or love, and send it in a text. Some of these would already be saved on my phone that I could simply copy and paste. I would write about things I remembered from the past, and the feelings of respect, gratitude, and love would naturally come, giving me guidance and inspiration.

## Aware and Awake

You see, the process of daily messages will start to cause a man to become aware and awaken him to see the good in the people he is messaging. This flows on to awaken his awareness of the good inside himself. We get so caught up in the hustle and bustle and the day-to-day grind of life that it's easy to let go of the people inside our lives without realising it. We don't think for a second about what it would be like for those people to hear that we do actually care.

Think of your relationships like a bank account. If you were to just keep making withdrawals, soon all the money would be used up, and there wouldn't be anything left. On the other hand, if you were to make regular deposits into your bank account, it would constantly grow and improve. By sending a daily text message to someone, you fill up that bank account between the two of you. The level in this bank account is fully determined by you and your ability to keep it topped up with your daily deposits of respect, gratitude, or love. Your relationship bank account level directly impacts the light that's lit between the two of you.

This is so simple and effective, with you having 100% of the power and control. There are men I've worked with who, like me, have changed and completely turned around their relationships with a daily message of respect, gratitude, and love.

### *No Response Required*

This is the first line of every message I send. This isn't about sending texts for you to get a reply, looking for approval and validation from them. It's for you to send a message with the only intention of filling up the relationship bank account and allowing you to say exactly what you want to say at that moment. If you expect a reply or get disheartened if they don't reply, you are not doing it for the right reasons. This is exactly why we do it by text message. For those of you who might be thinking,

### Shouldn't I Tell Them Face to Face?

No, this will require the person to have a conversation with you. We want them to see it, read it, and not have any obligation to reply. Don't think if they don't reply, then they didn't see it. Trust me, they have seen it, and they have read it.

Sending a text instead of in-person allows you to get deeper into what you want to say. Especially when you are starting, and if expressing your respect, gratitude, and love to someone is something you have never done before, it might be hard for you to actually say it to them. The other person might not know how to take it, which might scare them as they try to figure out what you are trying to do.

When this daily text message became a task I was committed to doing every day, I didn't spend too much time in my hometown where most of my life's important people lived. I was constantly working in different locations all around Australia. Sending this message allowed me to stay connected while I was away and strengthened my relationships without me even being there. I would come home, and that light would be shining brighter than ever.

Out of all the Daily 8 elements, this one was the last and the hardest for me to take on. There was a long time from those first videos I sent to the time I made this a daily practice. I kept telling myself I should start doing it, but my mind would immediately shut down that thought with the story that it won't make much of a difference and how I could possibly think of something new every day.

Maybe you feel the same way or are nervous about how it will be taken. If the relationship you want to work on has been tested previously from a falling out or is even just one step away from divorce or break-up. In that case, this can feel like a big decision to make due to the fear that it might push things over the edge. I take you back to Law #4: Trust... The... Process...

I can tell you stories of the men who start down the path of fixing their relationships with just a text message. Only a week later, their relationship is in a completely different state. I can also tell stories of the men who had to persist for over three months to notice any impact on their relationships. The important thing is to just keep showing up, keep making the deposits into the relationship bank, and keep trusting the process.

### Respect, Gratitude and Love

It all comes back to respect, gratitude and love. Reminisce about past experiences, and you'll be guided in what to write. What you will discover concerning your partner, wife, girlfriend, or significant other is that you'll find deeper reasons as to why you are with that person in the first place. It's not uncommon to send these messages for two, three, or four weeks, only to find that the person you are with is not actually the person you want to spend your life with. Don't let this scare you away from sending a text with the fear that you might separate; do this with the thought that you will find what it is that you truly want. It's something that will slowly grow inside you as you awaken the knowledge of what it is that you do or do not wish to continue.

When you take from your own life and give to others, you start to gain a sense of fulfilment and joy in your own life. This will increase your confidence and ability to connect and build relationships in the future. A big difference I found was that it allowed me to first notice the good in people. Even greater, it allowed me to notice the good in myself.

## KEY POINTS

**POINT #1:** The process of daily messages will start to cause a man to become aware and awaken him to see the good in the people he is messaging. This flows on to awaken his awareness of the good inside himself.

**POINT #2:** We get so caught up in the hustle and bustle and the day-to-day grind of life that it's easy to let go of the people inside our lives without realising it.

**POINT #3:** Think of your relationships like a bank account. By sending a daily text message to someone, you fill up that bank account between the two of you.

**POINT #4:** Sending a text instead of in-person allows you to get deeper into what you want to say.

**POINT #5:** It all comes back to respect, gratitude and love. Reminisce about past experiences, and you'll be guided in what to write.

**POINT #6:** When you take from your own life and give to others, you start to gain a sense of fulfilment and joy in your own life.

**POINT #7:** Firstly, you'll begin to notice the good in others, then it'll allow you to notice the good in yourself.

# 32

## THE DAILY 8: #6

### AFFIRMATIONS

*"You can't connect the dots looking forward; you can only connect them looking backwards. So you have to trust that the dots will somehow connect in your future. You have to trust in something - your gut, destiny, life, karma, whatever. This approach has never let me down, and it has made all the difference in my life."*
**- Steve Jobs**

Growing up, I believed I was shy. I believed I wasn't confident, and I also believed that I couldn't talk to girls. Why did I have these beliefs, and why did I believe them so strongly? Because I was telling myself these things nearly every day.

Not only were these lies and stories, but they affected the way I lived my life until I was about 25. The only time I felt confident was after a skin full of Vodka Redbulls or half a dozen Tequila shots.

Whether you're telling yourself stories as I was, you start to believe in these stories and simply accept that they describe who you are. This shows how easily negative beliefs can be formed. It's a vicious cycle that is very hard to break once you get stuck in it. The belief comes in, and because you are telling yourself that you accept it, your mind is already determining the outcome and reinforcing that belief.

In fact, in situations like those just mentioned, we already use our own affirmations. They might be far from positive, but they work exactly the same way. In order to change these stories you are telling yourself, we must add new stories that start shifting your beliefs. These new stories come in the form of positive affirmations that outweigh the negative stories and force them out of your mind and out of your current way of thinking.

When these affirmations get put on repeat, over and over again, inside your mind, they begin to take charge of your thoughts and stories. Which slowly changes your thinking pattern and ultimately changes your life and the way you act. Your thoughts are affected by the words you speak, so when the words and thoughts become aligned, then change becomes possible in your life and your reality.

I have an affirmation board in my bathroom for me to see and repeat every time I wash my hands, every time I brush my teeth, and every time I look into the mirror. I will not change this until it becomes ingrained into my unconscious and until I become the man that believes this thought to be true.

## Starting At The Bottom

To keep this as simple as possible. First, understand that everything is a learnt behaviour. Everything you like about yourself has been learnt, and everything you don't like about yourself has also been learnt. We don't have any of our current limitations when we are born. So you can see that everything starts somewhere.

Think about your name; you don't know what that is when you are first born. You don't even know the language; you just hear sounds. Our minds are smart, and we keep hearing this sound as people look and talk to us. Then, somewhere along the line, we believe that is our name. So my question is, where does that stop? I could write a whole book on this topic, and one day I probably will. But for now, just understand that all beliefs are started from a young age when you didn't have the logic and wisdom you do as an adult.

Put simply, none of these beliefs are true. They are formed in the unconscious mind to keep you safe and serve a purpose. Now you're older, they no longer need to keep you safe and are actually doing the opposite. This is when they become problems for you. These beliefs can be changed quickly when you know how.

## Rewiring Your Brain

Every thought you think and feel engages the circuitry in your brain, known as your neural pathways. In doing so, it strengthens these pathways and actually increases their size.

Neural pathways are the basis of your thinking, feeling, and acting habits. They are what you believe to be true and why you do what you do. As you practice travelling down new pathways, you actually weaken the old ones.[43] You start to weaken those stories you tell yourself until they simply fade away.

Thinking similar thoughts and feelings allows you to start creating new habits or reinforcing old ones. Repetition after repetition will lead to these new habits beginning to run on autopilot. This is when you know it's time to add another affirmation to your repertoire. There are no limits when you start to act in ways that support this new affirmation.

## Path of Least Resistance

We all run on autopilot every day through our unconscious minds. Your breathing, heartbeat, thoughts and everything in between are all done unconsciously. These neural pathways run on what is known as the law of least effort or the path of least resistance. This is the exact same thing that happens when you are driving to or from work, only to arrive, and you think, 'How did I get here?' or 'I don't remember driving here.' This is where your auto pilot comes into play and takes command of the situation.

Affirmations will start as one of the paths which are far away from the path of least resistance. With the repetition of these affirmations, you are training them to become at a place where they are on the path of least resistance. They will begin to be your go-to story, which is now the opposite of your previous one. This is the power of affirmations and why it's such a powerful addition to the Daily 8.

If you keep fuelling your brain with positive messages and new beliefs, even though they might not necessarily be true or correct at this point in time, you can begin to believe in these thoughts. Our self-talk becomes the reality, and we become our self-talk. If you keep flooding your brain with positive affirmations made by your mind, your brain will begin to believe them over time.

At first, it might seem like you are telling yourself a lie. This is somewhat true, but I like to think of it more as a command to grow. You are stating that this is where you want to be and who you want to become. Now you just need your body to follow. It's important to create a corresponding mental image in your consciousness of the man you demand to grow into. It then starts the subconscious process of embedding that image into your mind. In this way, your will starts to program your unconscious mind in accordance with your mental images.

The reality is that it comes down to the fact that most men have just never learned how to think and talk to themselves. Only recently have we become aware of the ability of thoughts to create our experiences. As our parents likely did not know this, it would have been impossible for them to teach it to you. The way they taught you to look at life corresponds with the lessons passed down from their parents. They were not wrong, and nobody is a fault here.

The time is now, and it all starts with you. You have the power to begin to consciously create your life in a way that you desire. To create the life you enjoy, you are excited to live, and a life that allows you to truly be the real man you are. You can be that man. I know you can be that man. It's time for you to wake up and activate him.

People argue and believe that affirmations don't work. I clarify that this has nothing to do with them not working. It comes down to their lack of understanding about implementing affirmations correctly to allow this transformational process to occur.

This is how it goes for these people. They might say something like, 'My confidence is growing by the day,' but then think, 'this is stupid and a waste of time, and it's not working anyway.' This second thought in itself is an affirmation, just in the wrong direction. So which affirmation wins out of the two? The negative one, due to it being part of a long-standing way of looking at life. It will take a long time for affirmations to work if these are said just once a day while you spend the rest of the day complaining.

What is done for the rest of the day is just as important as the affirmation itself. In order to have them work rapidly and constantly, it is necessary to formulate an environment that allows them to grow. Think of your affirmations as a seed planted in soil. If you have poor soil, you can only expect poor growth. On the other hand, if you place them in an environment with rich soil, abundant growth will occur. The affirmations will work quicker if you constantly think about the thoughts that support them.

### I Am On Fire!

There was a time in my life when I somehow started telling myself that I was on fire and that everything I did was on point. I unintentionally repeated this to myself 30-40 times a day. This was before I knew about affirmations. The more I told myself, the more I believed it, and I was getting twice as much done as my peers. I was asked a few times, 'How can you be doing so much more than everyone else and running at such a high level?' It wasn't clear to me then, but I now know exactly what it was. I was not only telling myself I was on fire; I believed it, and to re-inforce it further, people around me were noticing it and telling me.

This is not a hard concept, nor is it hard to implement. The struggle comes with your ability to start to believe what you are saying is true. Don't say it once; tick the box for the day and forget about it. Constantly implant this thought into your mind to truly reach the full benefits of the daily affirmation.

There's no need to create your own personal affirmation, nor does it have to be something that takes you a year to come up with. Start with something simple and meaningful to you right now at this moment. At the end of this chapter, I have added my personal affirmation that I have written on my board right now. Use it if you feel it suits you, and don't stop until you become it.

Affirmations can be hard to believe at first due to human nature, which requires us to see the evidence that something is working before we start to believe it. For them to work, we must change how we think.

The belief comes first, and the evidence comes afterwards to back it up. The moment you have faith in the not-yet seen, your reality will begin to shift.

## Brendon's Personal Affirmation Board:

Every Day, In Every Way, I'm Getting Better, Better & Better.

I'm Strong, Confident & Powerful.

I am Whole, I am Happy, I am Healthy, I am Wealthy, I am Helpful.

## KEY POINTS

**POINT #1:** We already use our own affirmations, but they might be far from positive.

**POINT #2:** In order to change these stories you are telling yourself, we must add new stories that start shifting your beliefs.

**POINT #3:** When these affirmations get put on repeat, over and over again, inside your mind, they begin to take charge of your thoughts and stories. This slowly changes your thinking pattern and ultimately changes your life and the way you act.

**POINT #4:** Neural pathways are the basis of your thinking, feeling, and acting habits. As you practice travelling down new pathways, you actually weaken the old ones.

**POINT #5:** The belief comes first, and the evidence comes afterwards to back it up. The moment you have faith in the not-yet seen, your reality will begin to shift.

# 33

## THE DAILY 8: #7

### MEDITATION

*"It's very important that we re-learn the art of resting and relaxing. Not only does it help prevent the onset of many illnesses that develop through chronic tension and worrying; it allows us to clear our minds, focus, and find creative solutions to problems."*
## - Thich Nhat Hanh

What is meditation? What is the point of meditation? How do we meditate? Why do we meditate? Does meditation work? Does it even matter? These may be some questions you ask if meditation is a new concept to you. I can tell you now that meditation does matter, it does work, and it is one of the most important parts of The MMC we strive to live by.

In 2019 I was introduced to meditation by a former mentor of mine. I had heard others talking about the concept of meditation, but I could never really comprehend it, and I certainly had no idea how to do it. Though it was already widely used by many inside the fitness industry who I had admired during the years previous, I still brushed it off as something that wasn't for me.

Whenever I heard 'meditation,' it always made me think of monks, and I had no intention of being a monk! Therefore, I did not need meditation. I imagined that meditation was just like sleeping and that, 'I meditate when I sleep.' How wrong I was on this...

Like me, you might be asking these kinds of questions or be stuck in a similar story. Or perhaps meditation is a completely new concept you have never even heard about before. Whatever the case, you should understand one thing: we don't meditate to get good at meditation; we meditate to get good at life.

There are so many benefits to meditation, and we as a society are only just brushing the surface on how it can change lives. I could go on forever about these benefits, but right now, I want to focus on just one: stress relief.

### Stress

Our body actually needs stress; it is healthy to have some stress. When stress hangs around for too long and doesn't go away, we start to experience some big problems. Most men don't consider themselves to be too stressed out, myself included. But when I said I didn't feel stressed, I was lying to myself. I just bottled it up and stuffed it right down. We all experience stress every day, from deciding what shoes to wear, what food to eat, how we will get the money to pay our bills, and what to do if we aren't able to work for a week. This all creates stress on our bodies.

Right now, men are walking around like little balls of stress and bottled-up emotions because nobody has ever told us how to deal with this shit. We are being brought up in a hyper-stressed day-to-day environment where everything is becoming a stress in our lives. This leads to the need for an escape from a source we know best. AKA alcohol, drugs, sex, porn, masturbation, working out, watching tv, a movie, gaming etc.

I didn't know how to cope with it. I also didn't know how to meditate.

When I first started meditating, well, what I thought was mediation, I went to the one place most people go to for 'how to' lessons: YouTube. I typed in '10-minute meditation'; I had been told that was long enough for beginners. I sat there with my eyes closed, listening to this video and following along with what the guy was saying. If any thoughts came into my head, I would try to turn my focus back to my breathing. The practice he suggested was simply to sit there in silence without any thoughts, to be in a place of nothing.

This sounded easy enough, and I was ready to dive in. When it came to being in that place of nothingness, I would constantly be overwhelmed with thoughts, stories, and ideas. Every time I'd try to return to the breath, my mind would shoot straight off into my next thought. I started to think, 'am I that messed up that I can't meditate? What is wrong with me? I can't do this meditation thing because I can't be in that place of nothingness without my mind going off on some strange excursion.'

I was meditating — or trying to meditate — because I was told it's a life-changing experience that would help me create some kind of extraordinary power in my life. ALL of the most successful men in the world are doing it. But I thought, 'well, I can't find this power and freedom in what I'm doing here, so I guess I'm going to go out and look for it instead.' I then began a quest to find out what this power and freedom really was that so many were talking about.

## Out of Body Discovery

This led me to a lady named Wendy Rosenfeldt and the ancient Indian meditation movement known as Transcendental Meditation, TM for short.[44] I was invited on a 4-day course which she ran about 45 minutes from where I lived at the time. Before the first session, I needed to organise two fruits and eight flowers to bring along with me.

So there I was flowers and fruit in hand, walking through a hotel complex looking for room 15. I wasn't sure what to expect at this stage, and it felt very strange, almost like I'd been ordered from some cougar meet-up website. Luckily it wasn't anything like that, though it was an experience that I still struggle to describe.

During that first session, I just stood there observing a ritual that Wendy was performing to a painting of Maharishi[45] while she recited the names of the gurus and teachers that were his descendants. Towards the end, Wendy started to repeat one word over and over. When I looked over at her, she signalled to me to begin saying it with her. It was later explained to me that this was to be my own personal mantra.

I was instructed to sit down. I kept repeating the word, more and more quietly, until it was just a mental repetition. Wendy then told me, 'Now close your eyes,' and this is where the experience began. Whoosh... I felt this big cloud of energy, power, and strength jump straight out at me from the painting of Maharishi. Shivers ran down my body, and I felt the hairs on the back of my neck stand up.

With my eyes still shut, the cloud began to fade after about 30 seconds, and I could see the room around me melting. It melted in waves, and all

I could see behind it was the shining light from the stars. Could this be what I was searching for: the light from what was melting around me?

I had been trying to meditate before this experience by blocking out my thoughts, trying not to think and just be. I learnt from TM that these thoughts are just vehicles for stress and don't have a meaning. Think of it like this: meditation relieves the stress we experience but doesn't remove it from the body. In order for the stress to leave our bodies, it must attach itself to a thought. This thought could be anything or everything. It's important not to take any notice of it and just to let it pass on by.

## Creating Space

What becomes possible is that meditation gives you the capacity to create more space in your mind when this stress is released. With this extra space, your mind can focus on the more important tasks instead of just fighting the stress fire. You will be able to gain clarity, confidence and courage that you may have never experienced before.

When we are stressed, the stress takes up all of this space and even tries to jam more of itself inside when we are already full. However, the more overwhelmed we are by stress, the less we see it. Stressed-out men do some dumb shit, and stressed-out men make some shit decisions, wreaking havoc on our minds and creating so much extra unnecessary chaos in our lives.

To take you back to the point where I said we need stress: the point is not to eliminate stress. Eliminating stress is impossible. We are always creating stress on our bodies in some shape or form, which is why the practice of meditation is a continual effort. As the saying goes, diamonds are formed under stress and pressure.

Meditation allows for releasing stress, which is how it gives you power. For most, having a few beers after work, working out, or having a few good puffs of weed can temporarily relieve you from this stress. But guess what? This doesn't prevent it from coming back after that suppression wears off.

## Shift in Perspective

Right now, your body can only handle so much stress, and this is limiting your capacity to get more done. This is why we must shift the mentality from 'I'm stressed; I'm going to drink' and shift it towards the new perspective of 'I'm stressed; I'm going to meditate.'

This sedation game, which so many men fall into, is the only choice guys think is available to them. Because we are never taught about meditation, we look for ways to sedate ourselves: working out, sex, drugs, alcohol, work, watching countless Facebook videos, drooling over IG models, gaming, falling victim to YouTube's algorithm and watching a whole series of Netflix. The only thing this is doing is masking the stress.

Sometimes this stress builds up so much and becomes so heavy that it seems the only thing to do is sedate yourself to escape it. I can tell you that it's even more important to create that shift in your perspective when you feel stressed out. This stress constricts your brain's capacity and ability to deal with everyday life.

Why do so many men get triggered so easily? Why do they end up with so much rage? Enough rage to make them want to chase a car down and beat the shit out of a guy just for cutting them off a few hundred meters back? This stress has consumed your capacity for space and your ability to deal with the trigger. So, the trigger is activated in direct response to this stress. Your actions might have nothing to do with the trigger, but the effect is the same. After this fit of rage calms down, the first thought that occurs is, 'Where the heck did that come from?'.

I had always been an internal rage-combuster – yes, that's a new word. I would get so frustrated at the smallest things, but nobody saw this. It was internal, and I would beat myself up for feeling this way. It wasn't until about a week after I had fully committed myself to daily meditation that my internal rage began to fade. I felt calm, had a heightened level of patience, and was consistently happier.

Nowadays, I religiously meditate for 20 minutes once or twice a day, once first thing in the morning and again in the afternoon. If I want to meditate on something I'm working on or through, I'll add a third session. When I emerge, I am on fire, sharp, and more awake than ever. If I were to turn to alcohol instead, I'd be dull, and I'd be even more tired. Meditation takes us from a place where we let the mind master us to one where we are the masters of the mind.

### The Quest for Cosmic Consciousness

I learned the concept of cosmic consciousness through which transformation can take place. It is a place where everything you have previously considered 'you' can be seen clearly, like looking through a piece of glass. The current 'you' is really just a state of consciousness determined and driven by the ego. Cosmic consciousness allows the mind to establish the unbounded awareness between our thoughts, feelings, and emotions. Over time, the stresses of the everyday grind of life cloud our awareness and begin to impede our capacities. When we meditate, it allows us to finally begin to function normally. From here, this lays the foundation for which your abilities as a man, a producer, and a provider, can experience transformational levels of growth. This growth allows the nervous system to refine and develop, unfolding your true capabilities and a great sense of love, appreciation, and happiness.

During my third session in TM training, Wendy described this state of consciousness as taking about 10-15 years for the average person to reach. If meditation is something you've never done before, you might think this is too much of an investment of time. From my short few years of meditating, I can tell you that you are missing out on life if you're not meditating. I will reach this state of consciousness, and my hope for you is that you take this on board and also commit yourself to reach this place. If you choose not to, that's fine, but I'll be sure to tell you what it's like when I reach the new heights it will allow me to reach.

I've had some intense experiences while meditating, but I've also had some practices that seem intensely boring. I've fallen asleep, spent the whole time looking at the clock every 15 seconds, and thought about what I'm having for dinner. I've even been completely deep in the zone, only to realise that I was in that zone, thereby kicking myself out of it.

I want you to understand that the quality of the meditation practice is not as important as simply showing up and consistently getting it done. Even if it feels like you're not getting anywhere and your thoughts are running rampant in your mind, you will eventually start making a noticeable difference to your life and your capacity to create.

Before we wrap up this chapter, I want to give you a suggestion for meditating on something in your life that you're working or working through. It's all about asking for help with the answers from the divine power and the universe. Set the intention by asking questions, such as 'How do I deal with ...?', 'What should I do about...?' or 'Where do I find...?'. Allow yourself the opportunity to create a space of clarity and connection, and see what answers come to you.

### Getting Better At Life

Meditation is a tool we use to release stress, create space, and become better at 'life'. If I meditate, I become great at life. When I suppress and hide this stress, I become overwhelmed, and my life crumbles around me. This is why meditation is not something that we should or have to do. It's something that we must do and something that we can become used to doing. It is a form of daily inner work, and you should know by now that inner work is the true way to move forward with your life.

There's no right or wrong way to meditate, there's no set time limit or times per day, and there are no rules. All that matters is that you do it to see massive results in your life. Is it hard? No. Is it easy? Also no. This is why it's called a meditation practice. Once you begin to hear the silence, the thoughts become so noticeable inside your mind. Quieten your mind and connect with your inner voice. When you meditate, you get 1 point for the day. Meditation is meant to do one thing: make you great about life, just like the MMC as a whole is designed to do.

## KEY POINTS

**POINT #1:** We don't meditate to get good at meditation; we meditate to get good at life.

**POINT #2:** What becomes possible is that meditation gives you the capacity to create more space in your mind when this stress is released. With this extra space, you will be able to gain clarity, confidence and courage that you may have never experienced before.

**POINT #3:** Meditation allows for releasing stress, which is how it gives you power.

**POINT #4:** For most, having a few beers after work, working out, or having a few good puffs of weed can temporarily relieve you from this stress. But this doesn't prevent it from coming back after that suppression wears off.

**POINT #5:** Meditation takes us from a place where we let the mind master us to one where we are the masters of the mind.

# 34

# THE DAILY 8: #8

## NIGHTLY RITUAL

*"When you arise in the morning, think
of what a precious privilege it is to be
alive - to breathe, to think, to enjoy, to
love."*
**- Marcus Aurelius**

It's Monday morning, your alarm goes off, and you wake up, still tired.
Is it really time to get up already? You give in to the snooze button and
try to cram in as much remaining sleep as possible, hoping that the next
10 minutes will somehow equate to 3 hours of sleep. Unsurprisingly,
you wake up even more tired than before, achieving nothing more than
just making yourself late. You get to work just on time, and because you
didn't have time to make your lunch in the morning, you walk to the
local café for lunch. Returning home after what felt like a long day, you

have dinner, maybe crack open a beer, watch a bit of TV or a movie and then head to bed — only to repeat the cycle every... single... day...

Sadly, this is what many men's mornings looked like before committing to the MMC, mine included. It was a cycle I couldn't break; I would constantly wake up hating my life. I was a carpenter for my entire working life before embarking on the AMD movement. Working in construction meant early mornings, early starts, and long 10-12 hour days.

Going through school, my mother would always make my lunches, so all I had to do was get them out of the fridge and off I'd go. Once I finished high school, that task was passed onto me, and rightly so. I would wake up, get dressed, and attempt to make lunch from whatever was in the fridge, all while scoffing down some cereal. If I was running late, I ate a pie for breakfast, and if there was nothing in the fridge, I went to the shop for lunch.

It took me about a year of doing this before I learnt a lesson from my father. He would always make his lunch the night before. At first, I found it a hassle, but over time it became a habit and a nightly ritual before going to bed. While my diet was improving, my energy throughout the day was also increasing, allowing me to actually start enjoying my workdays — all from *just* making my lunch the night before.

It wasn't until later in my life that I decided to add increasingly more small tasks to my nightly ritual and began to experience more big improvements.

### Own the Morning = Win the Day

There's no doubt that if you start your morning off on the right foot, then the chances of you winning the day have increased tenfold. If your mornings look similar to the situation at the start of this chapter, how likely is it that you will win the day? How likely is it that you will be able to give 100% in what you are doing if you are still playing catch-up from the morning? How are you going to manage to feel happy and energised throughout your day? The secret to owning the morning is to prepare for the win the night before.

The nightly ritual to the Daily 8 is the secret addition: the stuff that isn't fancy and that nobody sees, but it sets you up to win and hit all your targets for the following day. How can you be on fire if you are stuck in a war with the snooze button!

The idea of setting a nightly ritual is more than just setting yourself up to get enough sleep, which is what most men think of when I first suggest they set up a routine. Sleep is important and is definitely part of the process, but there are so many more elements inside this game than just getting enough quality sleep.

There is a lot of hype around what you should and shouldn't be doing at night or before bed to optimise sleep. I'm not going to bore you with the reasons as to why you need to get sleep; you can google that later if you must. People can get so caught up in finding the next 'hack' instead of focusing on the basics, on the stuff that works, like going to bed on time.

### Plan and Prepare

The purpose of the nightly ritual inside the Daily 8 isn't based on sleep. It's more about preparing and planning for your duties the following day. Getting to bed on time is just a small component of the successful nightly ritual.

There are no two ways about this. If you do not prepare, you will not have the capacity and capabilities to handle whatever is thrown your way the next day. It is easy to be a weekend warrior and wake up on a Saturday morning and achieve so much before it even reaches 10am, despite this not being the case during the rest of the week. You cannot be a so-called weekend warrior and expect to build anything great or lasting.

Think about these two similar scenarios with very different outcomes:

Scenario #1: Johnny wakes up, rolls over, and notices the time... 'Oh shit, it's 7.30!' He 'forgot' to set his alarm last night, and now he is late for work. In a rush, he brushes his teeth quickly and gets dressed in his car. Johnny didn't get a chance to eat breakfast or make his lunch, so he needed to stop at Maccas for a double-shot XL coffee if he hoped to wake up. He finally gets to work without a minute to spare, all hyped up from the hectic rush and stress he has already gone through that morning. The boss says, 'John, I need you to cover Bob's work; he's called in sick.' Johnny sits there thinking, 'How the hell am I going to cover someone else's work when I had so much to do before this came along?' Johnny struggles through the day, drained and exhausted by the rapid shifts in emotion he experiences. Coming home, he only wants to sit on the couch and relax. Completely ignoring his partner, he finds himself stuck in the story of 'My day was terrible.'

Scenario #2: Johnny wakes up at 5am, has a big glass of water, puts some clothes on, and hits the gym. He has a great session and feels fresh and on fire. Not long after returning home, he showered, had his green smoothie, meditated, enjoyed his pre-made breakfast, and left his partner a gratitude note on the bench top. After already owning his morning, he rocks into work and has some social time with his workmates before sitting down at his desk. The boss says, 'John, I need you to cover Bob's work; he's called in sick.' Johnny has no problem taking on this extra workload. He is already on fire and doing more than everyone else in the workplace. Johnny completes both his and Bob's work and is finished for the day. Heading home, he greets his partner, and they sit down to a nice home-cooked dinner.

Scenario #1 shows a one-dimensional douchebag, scenario #2 a man living by The Code and winning every day with preparation through the game of the nightly ritual.

## The 7 P's

Proper prior planning prevents piss poor performance. Your ability to think, plan, prepare, and decide is the most powerful set of fundamentals you have access to within your mind. These allow you to eradicate procrastination, thereby increasing your production and daily productivity. The ability to set targets, construct road maps, and take relentless action directly alters the trajectory of your life. Doing so will unlock your mental powers, activate your creativity, and expand your mental and physical energy.

It is amazing how many people do not plan for the next day, and this certainly shows in their productivity and performance — or lack of it. Every minute you spend planning can save you as many as ten minutes when it comes to execution.[46] Therefore, if you spend 10-15 minutes planning for the upcoming day, you could save yourself between 100-150 minutes that would otherwise have been wasted. That is over two hours you can save just by planning for the next day.

What is even more powerful is that when you plan and make a list the night before, your unconscious mind works on that list while you are sleeping. This means that your mind is working on ways to help you get done what you need. It is not uncommon to wake up with a great discovery on how to do a task better, more efficiently, and in less time than you originally thought it would take. As the saying goes, 'sleep on it.'

Let's say you have a project or task that might take days or months to complete and, taken as a whole, looks like one great big mountain you need to climb. Instead of planning every step along the way, we can create chaos without knowing where to start or having the exact outline that needs to be taken. It can be an hour or two every day that gets wasted trying to work out the task that needs to be done first.

When you begin to plan out every day the night before, you will find everything so much easier to get started and keep going. You will become faster and get into a smoother flow. You will get more done in a shorter time, which might surprise you. You hit your targets at a rate you had never thought possible. You will feel more powerful and more capable in everything you do, and eventually, you will begin to become an unstoppable force of a man.

## The Non-Negotiables

When constructing your nightly ritual, three non-negotiables must be included. Think of these as the foundation you are building to allow you to get everything done. They are; 1# prepare your ingredients for your green smoothie, 2# prepare your breakfast and lunches, 3# know your wake-up time, and more importantly, follow your set bedtime. We now add extra elements that you can do to make sure you are set up for winning the game for the next day.

## Eat That Frog

I was reading the book *Eat That Frog,* in which the author Brian Tracey discusses 21 different ways in which you can get more of the important things done today.[47] He goes on to say that the biggest task for the day should always be attacked first. Whether it be a hard task, a long and time-consuming task, or both, get that one done first.

For a long time in my life, I would do the complete opposite, and I know it's the same for many other men out there too. We tend to do the smallest and easiest tasks first to get them out of the way and to seem as if we are achieving so much while neglecting that big task, hoping that somehow it will magically get done for us. Think back to a school, college or university assignment. You might have weeks and weeks to complete it, but it keeps getting pushed back and put off until that last week when you think, 'Oh shit, it's due tomorrow.'

That one big task is generally the one that will make the biggest impact on our lives and produce our best results. Unfortunately, we still tend to constantly put it off. This is where you can see other men, or maybe yourself included, constantly seem so damn busy but never seem to be getting anywhere. More often than not, they are the ones who are not attacking that biggest task first.

Study after study after study shows that men and women who get paid higher and promoted quicker are the ones that drive straight into those harder tasks and the task that are going to provide the biggest results. This doesn't just relate to your professional life and career; it also relates to everything you do inside your life. I have the biggest and most important task for my health and fitness, another for my business and the third one for my relationships. These are all the targets I've set to complete as my first tasks for the day.

To recap, your 10-15-minute nightly ritual should include the three non-negotiables, prepare a smoothie, prepare breakfast and lunch and get to bed on time. To this, we add in the list of your biggest and most important tasks for the next day in the order they should get done with your most impactful one first. Doing so rounds out your day, prepares you to win and defeat your task and finally gives you that one last point for the Daily 8. If, at this stage, you have already completed the other seven elements inside the Daily 8, then you have become weaponised as a man, and as the provider, producer and protector you are born to be.

## KEY POINTS

**POINT #1:** If you start your morning off on the right foot, then the chances of you winning the day have increased tenfold.

**POINT #2:** How likely is it that you will be able to give 100% in what you are doing if you are still playing catch-up from the morning?

**POINT #3:** The secret to owning the morning is to prepare for the win the night before.

**POINT #4:** The nightly ritual to the Daily 8 is the secret addition: the stuff that isn't fancy and that nobody sees, but it sets you up to win and hit all your targets for the following day.

**POINT #5:** How can you be on fire if you are stuck in a war with the snooze button!

**POINT #6:** Every minute you spend planning can save you as many as ten minutes when it comes to execution.

**POINT #7:** Three non-negotiables must be included.

 1. Prepare your ingredients for your green smoothie,
 2. Prepare your breakfast and lunches,
 3. Know your wake-up time, and more importantly, follow your set bedtime.

**POINT #8:** To this, we add in the list of your biggest and most important tasks for the next day in the order they should get done with your most impactful one first.

# 35

## THE EXPANSION

*"It always seems impossible until it's done."*
- **Nelson Mandela**

Once the journey to becoming the Superior Man and rising into the king you are born to be is well underway, the next step is to add in the expansion and the systematic synchronising of targets to help you along the way. Specifically, daily, weekly, monthly, quarterly, and yearly targets along with monthly and quarterly benchmarks. As discussed in The GCG Chapter, we set targets and hit targets.

We don't allow any SMART goal-setting BS here. Leave that for the band of people who constantly set New Year's resolutions, only to have them fail by February. Not us and not this brotherhood. Targets get set, targets get hit, and the expansion of your empire increases.

What you get done in a day will make it seem like it's been a week. What you get done in a week will make it seem like a month. What you get done in a month will make it seem like six months. This is the power of targets; this is the power of benchmarks, and this is the power of expansion.

What becomes an addition and quantifies this effectiveness at a new level is what's called Reverse Manufactured Production (RMP). Essentially, this entails starting from the end and working backward, in reverse. After this is complete, we enter the manufacturing phase, which has been mapped out during the reversal process. Stick with me here, and let me explain in further detail.

As you have come this far, you should now know exactly where you are, who you are, where and who you want to be and what you want to become. This is done through the 2 'WTD' processes you should have completed during *Chapter 4 – The Path*.

For RMP, all we need to use from your 'WTDs' is WHERE you are right now and WHERE you want to be. Who you want to be and the man you want to become will become possible and attainable when you do the work inside the Daily 8, which we have already discussed.

To start with, you will go ten years from now and envision what you want your life to look like. Be clear on where you want to be at this time and what's going on around you. Note as many details as possible around what this all looks like to you and where you are. Most people underestimate what they can get done in ten years but overestimate what they get done in one year.[48] Knowing this, don't be afraid to go one or two or even ten steps over where you want to be.

Getting clear on where you want to be in these ten years already gives you an edge over so many men who are just moving through life, hoping this will work out. But that alone is not good enough here; we are chasing abundance and greatness.

After your ten-year target is set, we now move into the reversal phase. Come back toward the present and stop at the five-year point. As a general rule, this will be roughly half of what you have achieved in your ten-year outlook. Again, note what this looks like, where you are, and who you have around you. Be as specific as possible.

Coming back even further now, stop off at the one-year point. Again, be specific on what this looks like and where it is you want to be. This is where the first of your targets will be set. After reviewing where you want to be at this point, you will set out, as a minimum, three targets: 1 for your body, 1 for your relationships, and 1 for your career. Any other targets are added to this list.

Now, you have laid out a complete plan for your one-year mark. The final task is finding an image relevant to each target. It doesn't matter where these come from (Google, past photos of yourself, Pinterest, etc.). This gives you a very clear picture in your mind of what life will look like for you in twelve months, kind of like a vision board. Print them out, and add them to your Expansion Map.[49] This Expansion Map is a constant reminder of what you are working towards, and it is what will keep you accountable during your RMP phases.

In the second phase, the Manufacturing Phase in the RMP model is now used to map out and establish quarterly, monthly, weekly, and daily targets that will allow you to reach your one-year target. These targets are not as detailed as the one-year targets, and there is no need for images, but these must be realistic targets. For each of your one-year targets, you will have quarterly, monthly, weekly, and daily targets. If you have set five one-year targets, you will now break that down to five quarterly targets, five monthly targets, five weekly targets and five daily targets.

What you will find is that most of your daily targets will be included inside of the Daily 8. For example, if your one-year target is to lose 20kg, your daily targets would already fulfil Daily 8 #1 and Daily 8 #2.

Your weekly target could be to lose 0.5kg, while a monthly target could be to lose 2kgs, and the quarterly target could be to lose 5kg.

That example should open your eyes to the power of targets. Losing 20kg in a year might seem like a huge challenge to most people, but it becomes realistic and achievable when you break it down into smaller targets.

Let's look at another example: a one-year target could be, 'I want to be in a committed relationship.' Your daily target could be messaging or responding to just one potential partner. Your weekly target could be meeting up with one new female weekly. Your monthly target could be to continue with the two best matches for that month. The quarterly target could be that you have six potential partners with whom you are spending time. Along with this quarterly benchmark, you could add Daily 8 #6 as your new daily target.

Setting your targets clearly and spending time initiating their systematic synchronisation lays the foundation for success and expanding your empire. This might seem like a lot of work, and you might already be thinking about not doing this. Ultimately, the choice is yours. I can't do the work for you, and I can't make you set these targets, just like I can't turn you into a Superior Man. You do the work with the guidance this book has to offer and the tools I have given you. When you do the work, the work works. Stay true to Law #4 – Trust The Process and Do The Work.

You have now laid the foundation of the first phase, the Reversal, from your ten-year targets down to your first yearly target. From that, the second phase, the Manufacturing Phase, has been established, giving you a clear outline and plan of your quarterly, monthly, weekly and daily targets, which need to be met. You have your path, plan, and targets, all of which are laid out in front of you, and you just need to execute and hit those targets.

This is where the final phase, the Production Phase, is introduced, along with the monthly and quarterly benchmarks. This phase all comes down to the actions you take. The successful execution of these targets is where your production level will be noticed. The more targets that are met, the higher your production will be, which is measured by these two benchmarks. After the first month, you will review your one-month target and if it has been met or not. Changes will need to be made if it hasn't. For the most part, if these targets haven't been met, it comes down to your ability to execute.

The quarterly benchmark goes into more depth; a full review is conducted into the level of effort you have put in and the adherence to The 4 Laws, The 4 Pillars and The Daily 8. If your quarterly target hasn't been met, you'll find more often than not that this is because one or more of these aspects of the MMC haven't been met. This isn't a time to start shaming and blaming. We are simply laying out the facts of the last ninety days. The purpose of these benchmarks is for you to continuously track your results.

This is why so many goals remain just a dream; something people are only hoping to reach. Hopes and dreams rarely come true, so that's why this Reversed Manufactured Production model is so powerful. It turns the impossible into possible and the unreality into reality. Probably the most important part of all this is that everything you have established and laid out has now gone from a 'possibility' to a 'certainty' that it will happen, with you successfully executing and hitting all your targets. No more lack of direction or purpose, like so many men seem to experience.

### The 80/20 Rule

This rule simply means that 20% of your activities will equal 80% of your results, and 20% of your tasks will equal 80% of what you can achieve.[50] So, if you have a list of ten things you want to do, two of those ten things will turn out to be worth so much more to you than the remaining eight tasks put together.

Over time and as you advance through the RMP model, it will become clearer what these most productive and higher producing 20% targets will be. These are the targets you put most of your effort into and the ones you complete first. This is why you often find so many 'busy' people around, but they still don't seem to get anywhere. Year after year, they are still doing the same thing they have been doing for years. This comes down to the fact that they are stuck in the habit of doing all those 80% tasks and neglecting or putting off the 20% tasks. Generally, because these tasks take a higher effort to complete, it will not take any extra time to complete a 20% task as it would an 80% task.

When AMD was in its early stages, my entire life was busy. I was busy with these 80% tasks that were getting me nowhere. After a few months of this, I'd had enough, and I was nearly ready to throw in the towel. Everything in my life was great, and I was happy, but this whole teaching other men thing just wasn't working out for me.

That is until I stumbled across an article one day that introduced me to the concept of the 80/20 rule. It was a Friday evening; I had already decided to spend the weekend completely work-free, which was the best thing that could have happened to me. I returned on Sunday and told myself I had one more week, and if I couldn't see results, I was out.

### 'What is The One Thing I Can Do to Get Results?'

This was the question I asked myself that Sunday evening, so for the next week I only focused on that one area and nothing else. A week later, I had two new clients. At this point, I slowly started to develop the aspects inside the RMP model and everything in this conversation around The Expansion.

As tempting as it might be to clear up the small and easy tasks first, resist this and spend more time on those small tasks, habits, and areas that will produce 80% of your results. This can really generate a massive shift in your career and life. Not only will you have better results, but you'll have more time to do the things you want and love to do. Your top 20% will come to light during your quarterly benchmark reviews and will allow your expansion to increase at an accelerating rate.

## KEY POINTS

**POINT #1:** The next step is to add in the expansion and the systematic synchronising of targets to help you along the way. Specifically, daily, weekly, monthly, quarterly, and yearly targets along with monthly and quarterly benchmarks.

**POINT #2:** What becomes an addition and quantifies this effectiveness at a new level is what's called Reverse Manufactured Production (RMP).

**POINT #3:** Start at your ten-year target. Get clear on what your life will look like.

**POINT #4:** Break that down into a five-year, a two-year and a one-year target.

**POINT #5:** At the one-year mark, find an image relevant to each target.

**POINT #6:** From that, map out and establish quarterly, monthly, weekly, and daily targets that will allow you to reach your one-year target.

**POINT #7:** If you have set five one-year targets, you will now break that down to five quarterly targets, five monthly targets, five weekly targets and five daily targets.

**POINT #8:** Hopes and dreams rarely come true, so that's why this Reversed Manufactured Production model is so powerful. It turns the impossible into possible and the unreality into reality.

# 36

## PART IV: THE SUMMARY

### THE DAILY 8

*"A hero is born among a hundred, a wise man is found among a thousand, but an accomplished one might not be found even among a hundred thousand men."*

**- Plato**

As we bring this Part IV section to a close, we have first laid a foundation for Part I, II, and III with the inclusion of The 4 Laws, The 5 Pillars, The Path, The Purpose and The Possibilities and everything else discussed. Now with the introduction of the Daily 8 and the tools you need to continue this building process. The sky is truly the limit.

The game of addition is simple; rather than removing the old habits, we add in new and more aligned habits that imbed themselves in our lives as something we do. With the addition and acceptance of these new habits, the old ones are removed. No empty spaces that need filling from some other place.

## 8 & 56

For every day you complete an element of the Daily 8, you'll earn one point, giving you a total of eight for the day. As we add that up over the course of the week, it will equal 56 points for the entire week. 56 points = you are a force to be reckoned with. You are in control of where you are going and who you will become.

## Fitness

When it comes to your workout, you choose which one will raise your heart rate and make you sweat. It doesn't matter what you choose as long as you choose. Your mind controls what your body does, not your body. Don't let your body dictate what you do; that's for your mind. Working out allows your body to be aligned with the fitness you need to keep excelling as a man. One point for your daily workout.

## Nutrition/ Fuel

Your nutrition goes deeper than just having your green smoothie for the day, but that's the starting point. For this, you'll earn another point. There is no set list of ingredients, so you have the freedom to create what you like, provided that it's one-third greens, one-third fruit, and one-third water. For the rest of the day, we view the food put into your body as fuel that will power your Ferrari. If you fill up with cheap fuel, that's what the Ferrari, aka your body, will run on.

### GCGs

Goals, Commitment, Gratitude.

The simple yet powerful statement that you complete each morning lays the path on which you get done what you want to get done. Writing out your target lets you be clear on what you want to achieve. By committing, you are declaring to yourself, 'This is what I want for the day, and this is what I'm going to do.' Lastly, find one thing you are truly grateful for that day, disregarding whether it's good or bad. On completing your GCGs, you now have another point for the day.

### Reading

You can never stop learning and getting better; the principle is simple. If you are not going forwards, you are going backwards. Reading a non-fiction book of your choice for just 30 minutes a day makes you a little over 1% better for that day. This is going forward is how you expand as a man, as a husband, as a father, and as a producer and provider. Completing your 30 minutes will land you another point for the day.

### Text Messages

This one simple thing changed every relationship that I worked on in my life. I realised what I like in people, what I appreciate about them, why I love them, and why I respect them. It also became clear to me which relationships I didn't want or desire to have anything more to do with. This doesn't just apply to romantic relationships. We are talking about family, friends, workmates, clients, children, acquaintances, and everyone in between. Sending these daily text messages amplifies your relationships and gives you another point for the day.

## Affirmation

Each day we declare to ourselves that the new man we desire to be is represented with the affirmation made each day. Write it on the mirror, sticky notes, write them at the same time as the GCGs, and constantly repeat them over and over in your mind. Do not stop until you believe what you are saying, and you will get there. This is not a game of doing it once just to get the point. We add affirmations to change your thinking and your thoughts. This ultimately changes your life along with another point for the day.

## Meditation

When we meditate, we create space. The more space we have, the more we can enjoy life instead of allowing it to be taken over by the stress in our lives. Even if you don't think you have a lot of stress, you do. Everything in life is a stress in some form or another. Meditating helps to remove this stress from our lives. Every day, I wake up and meditate before I work out. It allows me to find the space I need for the day. It doesn't matter what style you choose; the most important thing is that you are making time for it daily. You'll get another point for the day for meditating.

## Nightly Ritual

The final Daily 8 habit for the day and quite possibly be your actual final task for the day. Winning the day starts with owning the morning, and we own the morning by preparing the night before. This game isn't hard, but it can make a world of difference in the morning. It's like going into a meeting with all the notes and topics in front of you. It's like having eight weeks of workouts already planned out for you. It's like knowing exactly where you need to be for each class. It's called preparation. Win the night = win the morning = own the day. Each day you take 5-10 minutes to prepare the non-negotiable along with anything else you can before you go to bed. You'll get that 8th and final point for the day.

Look, my brother, this isn't always going to be easy, and you're not always going to feel like doing it, but it's going to be worth every bit of effort you put in. It's not complicated; it's actually quite simple. One of the simplest games to play that can expand you as a man.

Every morning, you have the ability to grab your life with both hands and take it to all new heights. No longer will you feel that life just happens to you as though you have no control over it. You are the dictator and the creator of your life; as the Invictus poem reads, 'I am the master of my fate, I am the captain of my soul.'[51]

### Trackable Results

Each week we'll have real statistics which we can use to measure how your life is going and how your journey is working, all backed by facts. You can reflect, 'Well, I only got 49 points this week; what areas did I miss out on, and what effect has that had on my life this week?'

As we come to a close, you now have not only the knowledge but also the ability to see and achieve the possibilities that we discussed right back in Chapter Two. You look at the Daily 8 as a lifestyle you choose to live as you enter into all four dimensions of living the MMC way. This becomes more than an option; it's a must, a ride or die, sink or swim, fail or succeed.

There is one more thing you need to do now: take the plunge. Take a big leap into the unknown, and give yourself permission and backing to do so; all it takes is one step. One step forward every day.

It's simple, not easy, but simple. If you have made it to this point, it means you have already put in the work to get this far, so I congratulate you. Most men won't get this far, but you have. You are committed to taking this journey and becoming the man you never thought you could be.

Welcome to the brotherhood.

Welcome to this journey inside the AMD Modern Man's Code,

And welcome to a journey that will change your life forever.

The End.

## KEY POINTS

**POINT #1:** We have first laid a foundation for Part I, II, and III with the inclusion of The 4 Laws, The 5 Pillars, The Path, The Purpose and The Possibilities and everything else discussed.

**POINT #2:** Now with the introduction of the Daily 8 and the tools you need to continue this building process. The sky is truly the limit.

**POINT #3:** There is one more thing you need to do now: take the plunge. Take a big leap into the unknown, and give yourself permission and backing to do so; all it takes is one step. One step forward every day.

**POINT #4:** Welcome to the brotherhood.

Welcome to this journey inside the AMD Modern Man's Code,

And welcome to a journey that will change your life forever.

# ABOUT THE AUTHOR

'The cost of not making massive improvements in your life far outweighs the sacrifices you will make. I've spent over 6 years and $100,000 getting out of a deep dark hole in order to transform myself into the man I am today.

Do you have the time and money to throw away trying to do this on your own?

Do you want to keep drinking, doing drugs, gaming, wanking, or doing whatever else you can to try and suppress and sedate what is actually going on in your life?

No?

Then with next to no time wasted, here you will find the blueprint to jump-start yourself into a better life.

This guaranteed system will fill in the holes left in the lives of men growing up.

No man told us to speak truths, control, or even express our emotions, how to become a king, and how to build an empire as well as anything else in-between.

That is, until now.

*I have discovered a systematic Code with proven success, which men can live by daily to take control of their lives; to DO more, BE more, ACHIEVE more, and HAVE more.*

*This is the system and Code I wish I'd had access to six years ago'.*

Brendon Giebel is the Founder of Advanced Men's Development. He trains, coaches and guides men and women through life-changing programs, courses and events. His focus is on helping men and women regain their personal power and excel in all areas of life.

After struggling in his early 20s and being one decision away from ending it all, Brendon spent 6 years climbing out of the dark hole he was in. He then went on to study as a Master Practitioner of NLP, Time Line Therapy®, Hypnosis, and human behaviour, as well as his ruthless obsession with figuring out why people do the things they do and how they can then change. He now has the processes to help others create rapid transformations in their own lives and is leading the way for men and women to become the most successful versions of themselves.

He has helped people free themselves from drug addictions, negative thought patterns, unconscious sabotaging behaviours and crush self-doubt and low confidence. As well as help them move through PTSD, childhood abuse, anxiety, chronic pain and depression, as well as weight loss, anger issues, fear, and shyness, to name a few.

Brendon is a driven and motivated individual with a big goal of building the #1 training facility for health wellness and personal growth in Australia and personally impacting the lives of 10 million Australians.

# NOTES & ADDITIONAL RESOURCES

1. Lao-Tzu, Laozi, *Tao Te Ching* (2016); classic Chinese text. It is referred to as the Laozi and is also known as Daodejing, Dao De Jing, or Daode jing, English translation; http://www.taoism.net/ttc/complete.htm
Dr. Wayne W. Dyer, *Change Your Thoughts - Change Your Life* (2007)

Amon Greene, University of Washington Tacoma, *The Tao Te Ching [Laozi] /Lao-tzu Metaphysics (What is existence?)* (2017)
Waley, Arthur and Wilkinson, Robert, eds. *Tao Te Ching*. By Li Er Lao Tzu. Ware, Wordsworth (1997)

2. By Frank Litsky and Bruce Weber, The New York Times, *Roger Bannister, First Athlete to Break the 4-Minute Mile* (2018)

3. Barrow Island is a small island off the Nothern coast of Western Australia.
FIFO is an acronym for *Fly-In-Fly-Out*, a mining roster for workers who fly in for a period of time and live in on-site accommodation.

4. The Chinese philosopher Lao Tzu said; "The journey of a thousand miles begins with one step".

5. The Progressive Era, a stage in American history between the 1890s-1920s establishing entrepreneurism; https://en.wikipedia.org/wiki/progressive_era

Child Labor Laws, Walter Trattner, *Crusade for the Children: A History of the National Child Labor Committee and Child Labor Reform in America* (1970);

https://www.history.com/topics/child-labor

The Industrial Revolution

Documentaries and specific areas within society affected by the Industrial Age; https://www.history.com/topics/industrial-revolution

Brief Encyclopedia description of the Industrial Revolution's inventions and shifts within society; https://www.britannica.com/event/Industrial-Revolution

Riis, Jacob. *How The Other Half Lives: Studies Among the Tenements of New York,* (1890)

Garrett J. White, *Warrior Book,* (2017) www.garrettjwhite.com

6. *Internet Pornography by the Numbers; A Significant Threat to Society,*

https://www.webroot.com/au/en/resources/tips-articles/internet-pornography-by-the-numbers

NC Family, *The Effects of Pornography,* http://ncfamily.org/pdffiles/The_Effects_of_Pornography.pdf

7. Margie Meacham, *Extended Adolescence—and What it Means,* Steinberg defines adolescence as "the stage of development that begins with puberty and ends with economic and social independence." Based on his research, it is beginning as early as 10 and continues well into a person's 20s (2015) https://www.td.org/insights/extended-adolescenceand-what-it-means

Spear, L. *'The adolescent brain and age-related behavioural manifestations',* Neuroscience Biobehavior Review, 24, 417–463. (2000)

8. Tim Challies, *Devoted: Great Men and Their Godly Moms*, (2018)

9. Multiple meticulous and comprehensive surveys of the research are discussed in the following two books;
Burgess, A, *Fatherhood Reclaimed*, Vermilion, (1998)
Blankenhorn, D, *Fatherless America*, Simon and Schuster (1996)

10. Gary Chapman, *The 5 Love Languages™ for Men: Tools for Making a Good Relationship Great*, (2016) https://5lovelanguages.com

11. *The Love Language™ Quiz* by Gary Chapman, https://5lovelanguages.com/quizzes/love-language

12. David D. Deida, *The Way of The Superior Man*, Sounds True, (2004)

13. David D. Deida, *The Way of The Superior Man*, Sounds True, (2004)

14. *'your woman will be more fulfilled with 30 minutes a day of undivided attention and ravishing love than with a few hours of your weak and divided presence when your heart really isn't into it.'* David D. Deida, *The Way of The Superior Man*, Sounds True, (2004) www.daviddeida.com

'15. *The only thing that matters in this life is what do you think about yourself when you're by yourself.'* Tom Bilyeu, Impact Theory, *The Ultimate Advice For Every Young Person (How to Succeed in Life)* (2022)

16. Alice G. Walton, *The Science Of Giving Back: How Having A Purpose Is Good For Body And Brain*, (2017) https://www.forbes.com/sites/alicegwalton/2017/07/

10/the-science-of-giving-back-how-having-a-purpose-is-good-for-body-and-brain/?sh=21462ab86146

The Cleveland Clinic, Why Giving Is Good for Your Health, (2020) https://health.clevelandclinic.org/why-giving-is-good-for-your-health/

17. Andres Pira and Dr Joe Vitale, *Homeless to Billionaire*, (2019)

18. Naina Kumar and Amit Kant Singh, *Trends of male factor infertility, an important cause of infertility: A review of literature*, PubMed Central, (2015)
https://www.ncbi.nlm.nih.gov/pmc/articles/PMC4691969/

19. Steve Biddulph, *The New Manhood*, (2019)

20. Caleb Jones, *The Unchained Man: Alpha Male 2.0*, (2014) www.calebjones.com

21. Bill and Rich Sones, *Strange But True: 95 Percent of Brain Activity is Unconscious*, The Oklahoman, (2018) https://www.oklahoman.com/story/lifestyle/2018/10/09/strange-but-true-95-percent-of-brain-activity-is-unconscious/60496296007/

22. Byron Katie, *Loving What Is*, (2002) www.thework.org

23. For exclusive access to the AMD App, go to www.brendongiebel.com/amd-app

24. Don Miguel Ruiz, The Four Agreements (1997) www.thefouragreements.com

25. *'Every day...there is an epic battle going on inside you. It's the battle between two voices in your head. I call them The Boss Voice and The Bitch Voice.'* Andy Frisella, *75 HARD: A Tactical Guide To Winning The*

*War With Yourself,* (2020) https://andyfrisella.com/products/75-hard-a-tactical-guide-to-winning-the-war-with-yourself

26. 1964, *The Collected Works of Mahatma Gandhi,* Volume XII, April 1913 to December 1914, Chapter: General Knowledge About Health XXXII: Accidents Snake-Bite, (From Gujarati, Indian Opinion, 9-8-1913), Start Page 156, Quote Page 158, The Publications Division, Ministry of Information and Broadcasting, Government of India. (Collected Works of Mahatma Gandhi at www.gandhiheritageportal.org)

27. What the Bleep Do We Know? *WTB is a 2004 film that combines documentary-style interviews, computer-animated graphics, and a narrative that posits a spiritual connection between quantum physics and consciousness. The plot follows the story of a photographer as she encounters emotional and existential obstacles in her life and begins to consider the idea that individual and group consciousness can influence the material world. Her experiences are offered by the filmmakers to illustrate the movie's thesis about quantum physics and consciousness.* https://www.youtube.com/watch?v=PcKWx-wJv3s

28. Shad Helmstetter PhD, *What to Say When You Talk to Your Self,* (2017)

29. You don't have to look far to find personal trainers at any gym to find most of them don't look as if they've set foot in the gym for their own gain. I have had other professional physiological service workers around me, both male and female, who have many issues that haven't been addressed. If these people can't do it for themselves, how can they do it for you?

30. Regan Hillyer, Serial Entrepreneur, Philanthropist, Energetic Coach and Global Speaker. www.reganhillyer.com

31. David Leon, International Best Selling Author, Investor, Entrepreneur. https://leonpropertypartners.com/

32. James Clear, Atomic Habits (2018) www.jamesclear.com

33. Elena Volpi, Reza Nazemi, and Satoshi Fujita, *Muscle Tissue Changes with Aging*, PubMed Central, (2015) Published in final edited form as: *Curr Opin Clin Nutr Metab Care. 2004 Jul; 7(4): 405–410.*
https://www.ncbi.nlm.nih.gov/pmc/articles/
PMC2804956/#:~:text=Muscle%20mass%20decreases%20ap-
proximately%203,to%20disability%20in%20older%20people.

34. Garrett J. White, Warrior Book, (2017) www.garret-tjwhite.com

35. Joe Cross, *101 Juice Recipes: Reboot with Joe*, (2013)

36. In March 2019, Frisella, who is not a certified trainer, dietitian, or licensed clinical therapist, introduced the concept of the 75 Hard Challenge on his podcast, Real AF, suggesting that it's a way to change your life for the better and lose weight. Frisella writes that 75 Hard is "NOT A REGULAR FITNESS PROGRAM." Rather, it's a "MENTAL TOUGHNESS PROGRAM" that he is qualified to teach based on his "20 years of intensive study and real-life experience."

37. Research by the University of Scranton, *Science Says 92 Percent of People Don't Achieve Their Goals*, (2016) https://www.inc.com/marcel-schwantes/science-says-92-percent-of-people-dont-achieve-goals-heres-how-the-other-8-perce.html

38. Research by polling organisation WIN/Gallup, *Global Happiness Survey Shows Fijians Are The World's Most Con-*

*tent*, (2015) https://www.abc.net.au/news/2014-12-31/global-happiness-survey/5994014

39. Emily Fletcher, Mindvalley Quest: The M Word, (2018) www.mindvalley.com
Doidge, N. (2007) *'The brain that changes itself. Stories of personal triumph from the frontiers of brain science'*, New York: James H. Silberman Books.

40. Deyan Georgiev, *How Much Time Do People Spend on Social Media in 2022*, https://techjury.net/blog/time-spent-on-social-media/#gref
Hebb, D. (1949) *'The organization of behaviour: A neuropsychological theory'*, New York: John Wiley and Sons.

41. *Internet Pornography by the Numbers; A Significant Threat to Society,*
https://www.webroot.com/au/en/resources/tips-articles/internet-pornography-by-the-numbers

42. James Clear, Atomic Habits (2018) www.jamesclear.com

43. Dr Kim Dr Hil, Neural Plasticity: 4 Steps to Change Your Brain & Habits, (2010) https://www.authenticityassociates.com/neural-plasticity-4-steps-to-change-your-brain/

44. Transcendental Meditation (TM), https://www.tm.org, Medical benefits of TM: https://www.webmd.com/balance/guide/transcendental-meditation-benefits-technique

45. Maharishi Mahesh Yogi (born Mahesh Prasad Varma, 12 January 1918 – 5 February 2008) was an Indian yoga guru known for developing and popularising Transcendental Meditation (TM), and for being the leader and guru of a worldwide organisation that has been characterised in multiple ways including

as a new religious movement and as non-religious. He became known as Maharishi (meaning "great seer") and Yogi as an adult. https://en.wikipedia.org/wiki/Maharishi_Mahesh_Yogi

46. Statement by Brian Tracy, *Eat That Frog,* (2017) www.briantracy.com

47. Brian Tracy, *Eat That Frog,* (2017) www.briantracy.com

48. Farnam Street Media, *Gates' Law: How Progress Compounds and Why It Matters,* https://fs.blog/gates-law/#:~:text=%E2%80%9CMost%20people%20overestimate%20what%20they,can%20achieve%20in%20ten%20years.%E2%80%9D

49. The Expansion Map is a tool used inside AMD to make the impossible become possible. It's the number one tool that has allowed me to achieve 3-5yrs growth in just 12 months. Got to www.brendongiebel.com/mmc-course for more information.

50. The Pareto principle (also known as the 80/20 rule) is a phenomenon that states that roughly 80% of outcomes come from 20% of causes. In this article, we break down how you can use this principle to help prioritize tasks and business efforts. https://asana.com/resources/pareto-principle-80-20-rule

51. Invictus Poem, William Ernest Henley, https://www.poetryfoundation.org/poems/51642/invictus

> *Out of the night that covers me,*
>
> *Black as the pit from pole to pole,*
>
> *I thank whatever gods may be*
>
> *For my unconquerable soul.*

*In the fell clutch of circumstance*

*I have not winced nor cried aloud.*

*Under the bludgeonings of chance*

*My head is bloody, but unbowed.*

*Beyond this place of wrath and tears*

*Looms but the Horror of the shade,*

*And yet the menace of the years*

*Finds and shall find me unafraid.*

*It matters not how strait the gate,*

*How charged with punishments the scroll,*

*I am the master of my fate,*

*I am the captain of my soul.*

www.ingramcontent.com/pod-product-compliance
Lightning Source LLC
Chambersburg PA
CBHW071957260326
41914CB00004B/834